MY FATHER,
MY TEACHER

WITHDRAWN

The Catholic
Theological Union
LIBRARY
Chicago, Ill.

MY FATHER,
MY TEACHER

A Spiritual Journey

by Nichiko Niwano

translated by
Richard L. Gage

Kōsei Publishing Co. · *Tokyo*

The Catholic
Theological Union
LIBRARY
Chicago, Ill.

This book was originally published in Japanese under the title *Subete wa Waga Shi*.

Cover design by Tadao Koyama. Editing, book design, and typography by Rebecca M. Davis. The text of this book is set in Monotype Bembo with Palatino for display.

First English Edition, 1982

Published by Kōsei Publishing Co., Kōsei Building, 2-7-1 Wada, Suginami-ku, Tokyo 166. Copyright © 1980, 1982 by Kōsei Publishing Co.; all rights reserved. Printed in Japan.
ISBN 4-333-01095-0

CONTENTS

CONTENTS

TURNING POINT

During lunch after a Rissho Kosei-kai executive meeting on January 14, 1980, I received a telephone call informing me that my eighty-one-year-old aunt Nao, who lived in Suganuma, had died. She had long been confined to bed with degeneration of the brain, and we were prepared for her death. Still, it caused me great grief. Suddenly there flashed on the magic lantern of my mind's eye recollections of the ten years I spent living in my aunt's home in my early youth. As I led the memorial services at her funeral, on January 17, for a while I was unable to speak for trying to hold back my tears.

According to official records, Aunt Nao married my father's older brother Teizo in April, 1921, becoming the wife of the head of the Niwano family. This was two years before my own father, Nikkyo Niwano, left the family village of Suganuma, in Niigata Prefecture, to seek his fortune in Tokyo. Born and raised in an isolated place in a region of long winters and deep snows, Aunt Nao was always a woman of tremendous kindness and consideration, as my five brothers and sisters, my mother, and I had reason to learn during the decade we spent with her and my uncle.

I have many recollections of that time. I have even written on numerous occasions about my family, my elder sisters, my younger brothers, my mother, and my father. But I stubbornly resisted all urgings to publish my recollections in book form, partly because of an innate dislike of talking about myself and partly because I wondered what real value such a book could have. My mother says I have always been very cautious. According to her, even as a toddling infant, I would stand with the help of a piece of furniture only after I had first tested its stability. Perhaps I am a coward. My wife somewhat harshly says I will not cross a stone bridge without tapping it beforehand to find out whether it is solid.

But in recent years I have changed to an extent that startles even me. For instance, I once found addressing large groups painful in the extreme. Now I not only speak but even sing in front of crowds. The Japanese custom of requiring each guest at a party to entertain by singing a tune used to embarrass me terribly. In the past few years, however, if someone helps me remember the words, I can regale a party with an old tune—not very well sung it is true— and then immensely relish the cup of sakè that follows the performance.

In 1970, my father gave me the Buddhist name Nichiko, which was officially registered as my sole legal appellation in 1978. This symbolizes the turning point at which I now stand, and from which I hope to develop through contacts with many people. I take the opportunity of this moment of change to offer this book—in spite of its immaturities—in the hope that it will have something of value for my readers.

PART ONE
TO THE COUNTRY

EARLIEST MEMORIES

Rissho Kosei-kai came into being on March 5, 1938. I was born on March 20 of the same year. In addition to three elder sisters, I have two younger brothers: Kinjiro, who was born in 1940, and Hiroshi, who was born in 1943. Kinjiro probably remembers our early times, when father still operated a milk shop in Shimmei-cho, Nakano Ward, Tokyo, better even than I.

With three daughters in succession, my father was eager for a son and told mother he would celebrate with fireworks if the child they were expecting then were a boy. When I was born, there were no fireworks. But he was so excited that he sent a telegram to the family in Suganuma telling them the good news. I understand how he felt. At present the father of four daughters, I wonder if I will be as excited as my father was when my first son is born.

Father gave me the name Koichi, which was considered auspicious. I am sure he was concerned about me. But in those days most parents were too busy to coddle or pay much attention to their children. To-day devoted fathers and mothers take intense interest in their offspring's education. But such was not the case in our day. Father was too occupied with other matters to have time for us. I do not remember his playing with us when we were small or asking to be shown our homework after we entered primary school.

His life as a religious leader was paramount. He had many children in faith demanding his attention. His work with his companion in faith, Myoko Naganuma (or Myoko Sensei as she came to be called), steadily gained momentum with the passing years. To have more time to devote to it, he had earlier given up his pickle dealership to become the operator of a milk shop. His most compelling interest was less salvation for himself and his family than salvation for as many other people as possible. We six children may actually have been a burden on him. Shakyamuni, the historical Buddha, considering the birth of his son an obstacle in his search for enlightenment, left home and family for a life of religious discipline. Ultimately my father took a similar course and became and has remained a man totally devoted to his religion and to saving other people.

The first headquarters of Rissho Kosei-kai was finished when I was four years old. At that time, we moved from Shimmei-cho to Wada Hon-cho, where it was located. But before then, I recall seeing father's milk cart parked in front of the shop from morning till night, not because he did not do his work but because he got up early in the morning to finish his rounds. Then, after devotional services upstairs at home, he disappeared on his religious affairs all day. At night, there would be meetings on the second floor of our house.

The front part of the milk shop was a low earthen-floored space. A step higher was a tatami-matted room divided from the earthen-floored area by translucent sliding shoji panels. Farther inward was a small room (four and a half tatami mats in area) where we children all slept. Spread on the floor in the traditional Japanese fashion, our bedding filled the entire room. Visitors to the evening meetings greeted mother then picked their ways gingerly among our pillows and mounted the creaking stairs. Voices—sometimes the loud voice of my father—could be heard well into the night.

One of my most vivid recollections from this part of my early life was a school field day that my father attended, probably because of my elder sisters. Parents took part in some of the day's events, and I recall very clearly seeing my father dash ahead of all competitors in a bale-toting race to win first prize. I do not remember what my sisters did that day, but father's taking the prize is deeply emblazoned on my memory. I was very proud of him.

I suspect the happiest year of my young childhood was 1943, the year before I entered primary school and the year before all of us, except father, left Tokyo for Suganuma. In 1943, I went with father to a hot-spring bathing place. In those days, bombings were already taking place in Tokyo. It was scarcely the time for calm pleasure trips. But ours was not merely an excursion. Some kind of rash had broken out all over my younger brother Kinjiro's body, and, on the advice of Uncle Rinzo, father took Kinjiro, my sisters Kyoko and Yoshiko, and me to a hot spring reputed to have therapeutic effects. Uncle Rinzo went along too.

We took the train from Ueno Station in Tokyo to Itsukamachi, in Niigata Prefecture. Never having ridden on a train for such a long time before, I could not take my eyes off the endless series of fields and the blue mountains, seen from close at hand for the first time. Everything was new and dazzling.

I have no recollection of what we did or ate on the train. But the food father and Uncle Rinzo prepared for us in our self-service lodgings at the hot spring is clear to me today. We had delicious slices of bright red tomato liberally sprinkled with sugar. Whole small potatoes swam in our bean-paste soup. We had delicious small pickled eggplants. In addition to these daily dishes, we sometimes ate raspberries from vines on the mountains behind our lodgings. We children accompanied Uncle Rinzo when he descended to a nearby village to buy fruit and vegetables. I still remember the novelty of munching a whole cucumber just picked from the vine.

The hot-spring bathhouse was spacious. The blackened wooden tubs were unpleasantly slimy on the bottoms. The greenish waters reeked. At night, as my father and I would sit in the tubs under an oil lamp, fireflies would flutter in and out of the room.

Since his rash was bad, Kinjiro was not permitted in the tubs. Instead, he bathed in a wooden vat filled with water from buckets filled at nearby bamboo pipes by father. To me, soaking in a tub, his naked body looked very big as he went about this work.

I was happy to be with him. He laundered my underwear and did everything else for me. I was perfectly content. Reticent by nature, I probably did not talk to him much, but lying on the verge of sleep in bed listening to him and Uncle Rinzo talking brought a kind of fulfillment.

Thinking back on it now, I realize my contentment was odd for the times. The war situation was growing worse daily. No doubt, father and Uncle Rinzo were talking about it and about the future of Kosei-kai as I lay happily dozing beside them. Shortages of food and other essentials were growing steadily worse. Young men were being called up either for military service or for work in factories producing strategic materials. Though I was unaware of it, at the end of our first week at the hot spring, Uncle Rinzo was ordered to work at the Nakashima Airfield.

As he explains in his autobiography, two years earlier, father too had been summoned to the Maizuru Training Camp at the Yokosuka Naval Base for a physical examination. Contrary to all expectations, he was sent home again. I can only wonder what might have happened had he been inducted and sent to the South Pacific or to China. The hot-spring trip I now recall with pleasure might never have taken place. Who knows what would have become of Rissho Kosei-kai itself?

To this point, I have talked mostly about my father because I have very little specific to say about mother as I knew her in my earliest years. She was always mother. She was as blessed and essential to me as the air I breathed. She bore the burden of planning and caring for three daughters and three sons in a family that was far from affluent. But worse for her than domestic difficulties must have been the hardship of living according to the lights of a husband who, for many years, day in day out, thought only of his religious faith and who was always more worried about other people than about his own family. She has my profoundest respect, however, because I have never heard her complain about her lot. I shall have more to say of her when I discuss the years we spent in Suganuma, the period when she saw to all our needs without assistance. I only came to understand some of what she must have gone through when I was an older man with children of my own.

DIVINE INSTRUCTIONS

In 1944, incendiary bombs were falling on the Yama-note residential district of Tokyo. Houses in densely built zones were being razed to prevent the spread of fires, and people were being evacuated to outlying regions or the distant homes of friends and relatives. Schoolchildren were transported to the country in groups for safety. In the summer of that year, when I had just entered Wada Primary School, my mother took all of us children to live in father's home village in the remote mountains of Niigata Prefecture. Father himself remained in Tokyo. Evacuation for safety was the ostensible reason for our move. I thought it was the only reason for a long time. Later I learned that our circumstances were somewhat different from what I imagined.

Myoko Sensei, whom I have already mentioned as my father's companion in faith, received divine pronouncements and guidance. For some time prior to our move to the country, she had been instructed to tell father that, because of the important role he was destined to play, he must separate himself from his family and devote himself entirely to spreading faith in the Lotus Sutra. For a long time, father resisted these instructions.

This was not the first time pronouncements—divine instructions—had been delivered to him. In both 1941 and 1945 he was called up for physical examinations pending induction, and on both occasions, divine instructions to the effect that he would return because of his importance to the Buddha's Law had been received and fulfilled. Beginning in 1942 divine instructions occasionally said that faith in the Lotus Sutra would spread throughout the world on the basis of Rissho Kosei-kai's work. In 1941 and 1942, fire was predicted to fall from the skies on the city of Tokyo, but, in 1944, assurance was given that no harm would come to Kosei-kai headquarters. Indeed it was said that if a bomb fell on the headquarters the whole of Japan would be destroyed. In the autumn of 1940, on the occasion of the first pilgrimage to Mount Shichimen, divine information said that nineteen people would participate. When the final count was taken, twenty people, including father, were scheduled to go. Then, at the last minute, one canceled.

Although several other people were qualified to receive divine instructions, important ones always came through Myoko Sensei. Father considered this guidance from the gods and from time to time requested instructions when important matters had to be decided.

As I have said, however, he resisted the instruction to break up the family because of his belief that peace in the family is essential to peace in society, the nation, and the world and that family is the necessary ground for the achievement of the Buddhist goal of perfecting the personality. But the instruction was repeated day after day with increasing severity. The following is what I imagine went on in my father's mind at this time.

He had already become aware of and was deeply reflecting on his mission as a religious leader. He felt that, whereas an ordinary man seeking his own personal salvation was justified in being concerned with his family, a man seeking to save others and the whole world was not. Such a man must abandon everything. Believing salvation of the world to be his mission, he walked his own path without glancing back at wife or children. His instructions were to follow the example of the Lord of the Law, Shakyamuni Buddha; to separate himself at once from wife and children; and not to allow them to be a mental burden on him. He realized that the teaching in the Lotus Sutra—"We will not love body and life, / But only care for the supreme Way"—meant he must make this great renunciation. I am certain that he explained this to mother and then entrusted us to his older brother and his wife.

Undoubtedly divine instruction delivered through Myoko Sensei strengthened and assured father in faith. Rissho Kosei-kai had just been founded. Times were delicate and important. Instructions first to send his family away, then to read nothing but the Lotus Sutra, and later to read either the sutra or the writings of the thirteenth-century priest Nichiren were a further test and a factor enabling him to become the Nikkyo Niwano of today, the president of Rissho Kosei-kai. Without these instructions, father, who is only mortal, might have achieved less.

From the ordinary, worldly viewpoint, his actions may be hard to understand. But they made our present happiness possible. Mother often says, "My attitude then was really bad. I realize it now. But those ten years of trial are the reason we are happy now." I am firmly convinced that as the history of our organization unfolds the truth of this assessment of father's actions will become clear.

IN THE COUNTRY

On August 12, 1944, the year before World War II ended, six of us boarded a night train departing from Ueno Station in Tokyo for Niigata. At the time, mother was thirty-six; my eldest sister, Tomoko—who remained in Tokyo to attend Rissho Girls' School—was thirteen; Kyoko was eleven; Yoshiko was eight; I was six; Kinjiro was four; and my youngest brother, Hiroshi, was one. We rode the Joetsu Line—with which I associated pleasant memories from the earlier hot-spring trip—and transferred to the Iiyama Line at Echigo Kawaguchi. At our destination, Tokamachi, a group of relatives waited to help with luggage and to carry the small children piggyback the six kilometers from there to our village, Suganuma.* Though winter is long and cold

*Officially Suganuma has another name: Saruko after the ape sign (*saru*) in Chinese astrology. Today it is called 15

in that part of Japan, the summer sun blazes. Mother's eldest brother carried me on his shoulders. Soon, when our road went uphill, he stripped to nothing but his loincloth; the sweat from his naked back soaked my clothes. Mother and my sisters walked behind us. My uncle finally put me down in front of the huge, old-fashioned, two-story thatched house that was to be home for a long time.

Inside the door I smelled cows. Indeed the cows and the human beings shared the same roof. To reach the toilet, one had to pass through the cow shelter, a trip I disliked and feared.

On a raised level inside the entrance was a hearth set in the floor. Above it from the ceiling hung a long, pitch-black pole with a hook on the end from which kettles and pots for cooking could be suspended. We were given the large, ten-tatami-mat inner sitting room for our use. In this new, strange place, we found much to amaze us. A flight of steps led up from a wooden-floored corridor to a room where there were many shelflike boards on which silkworms were raised.

My grandfather and my aunt's mother were the eldest members of the family then. In addition, my uncle (father's oldest brother) and his wife and five

Saruko, Tokamachi city. Indeed other nearby villages too have double names: Oike, where the primary school I attended was located, is called Toriko after the bird (*tori*) sign; Akakura, largest of the villages, is called Inuko after the dog (*inu*) sign; and Karusawa, where mother was born, is called Iko after the boar (*inoshishi*) sign.

children inhabited a building that, with the sudden onslaught of mother and the five of us, had to accommodate fifteen. This was a burden on my aunt and uncle and a great embarrassment for mother. Still, supper that first night was boisterous and fun. We children were fascinated by the unknown new life we were starting. Mother was much less pleased. She sat up for a long time that night discussing things quietly with our aunt. In 1945 my oldest sister, Tomoko, joined us in the country. An incendiary bomb had destroyed her school. I entered Oike Primary School when the second term began, after summer vacation. The schoolhouse was smaller than anything I had known in Tokyo, and the corridor floors squeaked under our feet.

When winter set in, as much as four meters of snow engulfed the thirty-two houses in Suganuma, forcing us to remain indoors and devise ways of passing the time—without the benefit of toys. Once my cousins made an imitation grain reaper out of a step ladder, harnessed themselves to it, and pulled it around the house, making roaring sounds to simulate machinery. Kinjiro and I stood on the sidelines shouting encouragement. The adults smiled wryly at the way we all copied our parents' occupations.

All of us children were growing, therefore, eating. Even for a farm family, this presented problems, especially since there was no money income and mother had no funds of her own. My greatest desire was to be of help to her. This prompted me to say "white-collar worker" when our teacher asked us what we wanted to be when we grew up. Although our teacher complained of my lack of ambition, a job as a white-collar worker seemed the ideal way to make money to bring some relief into mother's life.

My aunt was a gentle person. But my stricter uncle, naturally, as the head of the house, kept guard on the purse strings. I hated having to ask him for money for school expenses or supplies and usually got my sister Kyoko to do it for me.

But uncle was not a stingy man. It is true that, since rice could be bartered for practically anything we needed, money was scarce. Nonetheless at festival or school-excursion time, he always managed to come up with a little spending money that was a joy-giving blessing from heaven to us.

Several times a month he traveled to Tokyo to get money for our upkeep from father, though the amount was not always great. In 1948 work got under way on the Kosei-kai headquarters training hall. Then construction started on the Kosei Nursery School, the second training hall, and the Gyogakuen building, which now houses our seminary and our library. Father and Myoko Sensei were totally engrossed in this work with the result that sometimes my uncle received no more than two or three thousand yen on his trips to the city.

In the summer of our second year in the country, to reduce the burden we caused, mother took my sister Tomoko, my brother Hiroshi, and me to the home of her older brother in Karusawa. Our uncle from Suganuma loaded our baggage on a cow and accompanied us. But we had not been there long till one night I waked to hear mother and her brother quarreling bitterly. We returned to Suganuma forthwith. I had changed to the Karusawa Primary School on our move and had to re-enroll in the one in Oike when we got back.

During our stay in Suganuma, father visited us three times. The first was when he had to take his second physical examination for possible induction and came to say goodbye to everyone in the home village. The second was in 1948, when grandfather died. The third was when my sister Kyoko and my cousin Masatoshi Niwano married.

On the eve of his physical examination he had Myoko Sensei and other leaders of the organization with him. He said nothing to mother or us. In the evening the villagers came to give him a send-off party, as was customarily done for soldiers in those days. We were not allowed to draw near him. And something would not let us try. Of course, our experiences in the village may have converted us too into country children who hide at the sight of strangers and hang their heads when spoken to. But something else kept us away from him: a look on his face that awed us.

Of course, we wanted to see him. Kinjiro and I made holes in the paper of the shoji panels and peeped through at him from the adjacent room. On the following day, waving small Japanese flags and singing songs, we joined the crowd accompanying him to the shrine of the local tutelary deity. But that was as intimate as we got.

That trip grieved father, as I found out when recently, as chairman of a committee editing his lectures on the Buddha's Law for publication, I came across statements revealing his true feelings then and at several other stages of his life. I was especially touched by his emotions during his visit to Suganuma in March 1945. Believing induction a certainty that time, he regarded the visit as possibly the last chance he would have to see his family in this life. In his writings he says how he wanted to talk with us but exerted maximum self-control to obey the divine instructions governing him. Once again, I can only imagine how mother and father got through what might have been their last night together in silence. But they did manage.

As I have said, however, father was declared unfit this second time too. His examining officer said, "You have great work to do behind the lines. There is no difference in importance between men serving their country on the battle front and men saving people at home." Then he stamped "UNFIT" on father's report. After the initial shock, father immediately understood the full weight and significance of the reprieve and, moved by the Buddha's compassion, resumed obedience to the divine instructions. Five months later, the war ended, and Rissho Kosei-kai began its period of rapid growth and development. Father was thirty-eight at the time; I was seven.

Shortly after we returned to Suganuma from Karusawa, the engagement of my oldest sister, Tomoko, and the first son of the head family in the village—his name was Kenzo, and the head house was one minute's walk from ours—was announced. The wedding took place in deep snows on January 21 of the following year, 1946. According to the old way of reckoning ages, on New Year 1946 Tomoko became sixteen. This had bearing on the nuptials.

My father did not attend the wedding, though he sent a letter instructing Tomoko to hope for protection from her ancestors. His agreement to the wedding was slow to come and grudgingly given. I later learned that when the head house began looking around for a bride for Kenzo they consulted a fortuneteller in Tokamachi, who told them the family would prosper if the oldest son married a girl aged sixteen. This is why they were eager to arrange a match with Tomoko.

Kenzo was the family heir. The house where he and his new bride lived was already packed with people: his aunt and uncle, the heads of the family; his own parents; his six brothers and sisters; and his grandmother. To ensure correct family succession, six years after their marriage, Tomoko and Kenzo were adopted by their uncle and aunt. My sister then found herself in the complicated position of having to care for two sets of in-laws: her husband's true parents and his adoptive ones. The two older women did all the household chores, and Tomoko was forced to work in the fields with the men. I can imagine how difficult and bitter this must have been for a girl raised in Tokyo. But she never complained.

Only recently, she explained her feelings to me. "When I was in the third year of primary school, father used to write my name in my textbooks for me. In my fourth year, he stopped and never took care of me in any way again. Still, I didn't mind much. After we moved to the country, what with looking after brothers and sisters and all the other work, I didn't have time to think about myself. Like mother and father, we children had our sufferings to bear.

"I was very sad when the family told me I had to marry into the village head house but didn't have courage to refuse. Then I thought, 'Well, if this will make the others happy—' The years flew by. I remained in Suganuma, father's birthplace. And today it makes me happier than I can say to be able to serve faithful members of the organization who visit our village."

Tomoko has a far-perceiving eye. Even at that early time, she—and mother too—may already have understood father's mission. On this same occasion, we went on to talk about mother and her loving kindness, which enabled her to bear the humiliation of being treated as a hindrance by Kosei-kai members and to raise us children in spite of everything. Today Tomoko has two sons, two daughters, and five grandchildren. Her husband, Kenzo, is the director of the Kosei-kai Suganuma training center.

THINGS TO EAT

We had no idea what the rest of Japan was eating during our years in Suganuma, but our fare was of the coarsest. For breakfast we had dumplings made of rice and millet flour and filled with bean-paste. They were toasted over the fire of the open hearth. For special occasions, like the Yakushi Festival, the millet was replaced with mugwort, and the filling was of sweet red bean paste. With more than ten people to feed, rice was always served as gruel, which is watery and makes the grain go farther. To stretch it even more, it was eked out with yams or *daikon* radish. My cousins were sometimes so embarrassed that their lunches contained less rice and more filler than their schoolmates' that they refused to carry lunch pails. I remember covering my lunch pail with the lid while I ate so that people could not see what was inside.

Greens from the mountains—bracken, fern tops, and udo (*Aralia cordata*)—were important additions to our diet. In spring, when the snows melted and these tender plants put forth their fresh shoots, we children loved to go into the woods in search of them. Mother was most skillful at this task and often returned with a basketful of greens on her back. Sometimes this work gave us a chance to glimpse her, fleetingly and through childish eyes, in her lonely sadness. One day she went out gathering and did not return for so long that Kinjiro and I began to worry. After a while, we set out in the direction we assumed she had taken. As we went along, we called out, and finally from the distance her voice came back in reply. We saw her from afar, bowed under the load on her back. The sight was both an intense relief and a poignant revelation of the hardships she bore alone.

Incidentally, fern tops, which can be dried and stored for a long time, provided us with a source of money income. When I was in the fifth year of primary school, we decided to sell these dried plants in town for money to buy baseball equipment. The gloves we purchased, though cheap cloth affairs with a little thin leather stitched to the pocket, were treasures to us. It took me days longer to fill my quota of fern tops (a little under four kilograms dried) than it did the more skillful local country children.

Small amounts of seafood began to reach us the year after the war ended. Our first animal proteins were in the form of dried whale skin that could be cut thin and cooked with vegetables to make a warming, filling, winter dish. Another winter treat was hare. All the men in the village formed hunting parties to shoot or trap the animals, which we divided up and took home, where we pounded flesh and bones together on a flat stone with the head of an ax. Out of this, we made delicious meatballs.

Bean curd is a favorite Japanese source of vegetable protein. In the country, we made our own. Soybeans were soaked in water till soft then ground in a stone mill to produce soy milk from which bean curd is made. The stone for this work was light enough that we children could rotate it. The much heavier stones for grinding grain (especially buckwheat for noodles) were too much for us.

Once Kinjiro and I were fed weasel. The creature, whose strange cry we heard one morning, was caught in a trap set for rats in the vegetable-storage cellar under the kitchen. Country folklore claims that the flesh of the weasel cures bed-wetting. I confess both Kinjiro and I had been guilty of this misdemeanor in Tokyo and slipped up from time to time even after we moved to the country. This is why the flesh of the unfortunate weasel was given us to eat. I do not remember what it tasted like.

Berries, fruits, and nuts were treats in several seasons. In the summer we ate raspberries and mulberries. In the autumn there were grapes, purple *akebis,* chestnuts, persimmons, and silverberries (two varieties: rice-planting silverberries that ripen in the summer and harvest silverberries that ripen in the fall).

I suppose the one unforgettable food for me was

the curry and rice I ate at a bazaar at my sisters' girls' school in Tokamachi. The students had prepared it themselves. It was hot, but delicious. I ate every grain of rice and then relished the glass of cold water I chased it down with. Of course, we all had appetites of growing children, and the chance to eat curry and rice came seldom. And that particular dish has never again tasted as delicious to me as it did then.

Children living in Japan today, when practically anything is available to anyone, cannot imagine the poverty of our times. Still, I am glad I grew up then. Plenty is preferable. But it can sometimes warp the human personality if accepted in the wrong way.

As an agricultural people, for centuries the Japanese received the blessings of sun and rain, were sensitive to changing natural phenomena, and rejoiced and grieved with the passing seasons. Living together with nature, they know its harshness and gentleness. This knowledge cultivated in them a richer humanity. Sadly, today, living in a modern industrial nation, we have lost many of our old opportunities of coming into contact with nature. We are no longer grateful for nature. We no longer know how to rejoice at an abundant harvest.

Most Japanese people who are older than I experienced the poverty of the war and the postwar years. Though I hope none of us ever has to go through such trials again, I cherish their memory. Out of that poverty came the vitality of today. Few

33

young people now realize that plain rice gruel can taste better than the thickest, juiciest beefsteak. I know it can, and the experience from which that knowledge comes is precious.

NATURE'S POWER AND PROVIDENCE

Every autumn I recall the winters at Suganuma. Of course, I have recollections associated with each of the four seasons, but I liked winter best. Though the severe cold caused hardships, for some strange reason, the hardships of childhood are often later remembered with pleasure.

In late October, we built high fences of wood and straw mats all the way around the house to protect it from wind and snow, which began falling in the middle of November. First, snow from the mountains danced down on our village. Then heavier snowfalls started, and in the corners of fields and gardens some patches of white remained and refused to melt.

Sometimes the sun pierced the heavy cover of leaden clouds, but only briefly. Darkness always set in again at once. One evening we would be remarking about how snappy the air was, and the next morning a meter of fresh-fallen snow would have obliterated fields, the black earth of which would remain covered until April of the following year.

The weight of snow on roofs was so tremendous that indoor sliding partitions stuck in place. A house could be crushed under the load. Several times each year, families climbed to the roofs of their houses and shoveled the snow off. It fell to the ground, piling up on the snow already there, making walls from two to four meters high all around the building and thus raising our walking paths to the level of the eaves. These snow walls kept the insides of houses dim all winter.

Day in and day out, from the low, gray clouds snow fell and whirled wildly in howling winds, like sorcerers who invaded houses no matter how tight the shutters and sliding doors were shut. It was not unusual to awake to find a powder of snow on the tatami mats around one's pillow.

One of our chores was to go out early in the morning after a storm and trample a new path with our snowshoes. Each family was responsible for a certain route, and we all took turns making the kilometer path to the schoolhouse. On fair days, the walk to school was pleasant. In blizzards, it was almost too difficult to accomplish. Buffeted from all sides by the wind-driven, falling snow and by the ground snow whirled upward in gusts, with bodies bent double into the gale, we breathlessly trudged on. Getting bogged down in snowdrifts was frustrating enough to make me cry. But we had to go on— following the same path my father had walked dec- ades earlier. My first winter there, those trips were nearly too much for me. My feet were always unbearably icy when I finally reached school.

Winter made me sob many times, but I love both it and its severity. People from northern climes have a wonderful power of perseverance. Lips pressed together, eyes narrowed, and heads bowed, they make their ways through blizzards. They know the importance of the warmth each person contributes to a hearthside gathering when wind makes the snow dance outside and when huge icicles hang from the eaves. They all have the strength to endure and wait for the spring they know will come, sooner or later.

Severity and hardship of the kind winter imposes on people have a tempering effect on the human character. In the future, I may be called on to suffer and to endure. I believe that my childhood experiences with harsh winters have tempered me to withstand what I must. As I think now about winter, my mind is led to consider the members of Rissho Kosei-kai who struggle through snowstorms to take the Buddha's teachings to others.

My cousin Masatoshi Niwano, my Suganuma uncle's eldest boy, ten years my senior, is an example of this kind of person. In 1954, when a Kosei-kai chapter was formed in Echigo Kawaguchi, he became a leader. He was made assistant head of the chapter five years later. During the whole course of his work with the chapter, he commuted daily between Suganuma and Echigo Kawaguchi. To do this, he walked the six kilometers to Tokamachi

Station before dawn and then rode about an hour on the Iiyama Line to his destination. The return journey sometimes got him to his house at nine and sometimes not until eleven at night. He says, however, that the late-night mountain road held no fear for him because, as he walked, he constantly repeated to himself the Four Noble Truths, the Eightfold Path, and the Law of the Twelve Causes—all basic Buddhist doctrines. A classic example of northern-folk perseverance, he makes me realize how demanding discipline in the Buddha's Law is.

Now he is director of the Kinki Dissemination Area and of the Osaka Fumon Hall. In connection with this work too he has experienced trials demanding patience and endurance. At one juncture, intending to construct a new training hall, he had a prefabricated one erected as a stopgap. Then the plan for new construction was shelved, and he had to go on working in the ostensibly temporary building for twelve years. He says he always knew that the Buddha would make the necessary arrangements and, without complaint, conducted his training programs in the shelter he had. In 1977 a splendid new Osaka Fumon Hall was completed. His comment was: "Actually, I am by nature impatient. But I learned to endure from living in a cold, snowy part of the country. I am not aware of exerting special efforts to make the best of my situation; I simply didn't mind the waiting."

If life in lands of heavy snowfall has its hardships,

it has its pleasures too—pleasures that cannot be enjoyed in cities. We skied on homemade, cedar-plank skis, whose ends we heated and bent upward. We waxed them for smoothness and speed. Lacking anything fancy like modern ski bindings, we tied our skis to our boots with cord. To make our own ski slope, we trampled the snow hard. First trudging up, we then skied down then trudged back up again. We never tired of this, though it went on for hours on end.

When I was in the third year of middle school, my uncle—I think on my father's instructions—bought me a pair of real skis and ski boots on one of his trips to Tokyo. They were excellent for actual skiing but too heavy for walking and trudging up home-made slopes. Furthermore, though I was very happy to have them, I was a little shy because they were very different from the cedar-board skis my friends had.

New Year was always the highlight of the winter. As soon as the deep-toned midnight bell marking the end of the old year stopped ringing, we all got ready to make our first pilgrimage of the new one to the local Shinto shrine. Sometimes we bound our heads with towels against the sharp, cold air of a starlit night. Sometimes we covered them with straw hats and plodded through blizzards so thick that the footsteps of the person in front vanished the instant he made them. No matter what the weather, everyone exchanged best wishes in the exhilarating freshness of the first dark morning of the year.

The shrine of our tutelary divinity was a plain, humble affair. A moderately small room with straw mats on the floor and a small sanctuary at one end was illuminated by a single naked light bulb and votive candles. But, in my memory's eye, the building blazes with light and solemnity. I felt very proud and grown-up on these occasions because only men were allowed to participate in the rites.

After returning from our pilgrimage, we all went back to bed and slept till morning. Upon arising, we immediately turned to our first task of the year: twisting straw into a new rope symbolic of our willingness to work hard for the coming twelve months. Then, at last, came the New Year's meal and its special *zoni*—glutinous rice cakes and vegetables in broth. The first taste of this treat after New Year greetings exchanged afresh is something to look forward to.

During the holiday, young people went from house to house playing card games or *shogi,* which is something like chess. Smaller children played a kind of backgammon. We were all very happy because New Year was the one time when no one scolded us no matter how late we played.

This chance to relax completely was welcome in the country, where farmers work without rest during the growing season and in the winter, when they make footwear, raincoats, and broad-brimmed hats of straw for family use and for sale in nearby towns as a source of money income. We children were assigned the task of twisting straw into rope, a job that for some reason always gave me a headache. Although it was simpler and plainer than anything city dwellers can imagine, our New Year was a source of great happiness to grown-ups and children alike as a long-awaited respite in the crowded farmer's calendar.

A number of traditions and taboos are associated with New Year in Suganuma. For instance, on the fifteenth and sixteenth of January, called Little New Year, it is customary to eat roasted glutinous rice cakes topped with ginger-flavored bean paste. Some of these cakes must be offered in the family Shinto shrine first. Before that is done, strict taboo forbids anyone to put his feet into the hearth around which we sat to eat. I recall the shock I experienced when, as a newcomer to village customs, I violated this taboo and greatly angered my ordinarily gentle grandfather, who put great store by local traditions and observances. When he saw what I had done, he seized a pair of the iron chopsticks used for putting fuel on the fire and cried: "I'll break your legs for you if you don't get your feet out of there!"

On the twelfth of March, while snow was still on the ground, the village men conducted a ceremony to ward off evil at a mountain called Juniyama. We all took bows and special arrows made of miscanthus reeds and shot at a large, old cedar on the mountain. Each person whose arrow stuck in the tree, indicating security from harm, was overjoyed.

Finally, after half a year under snow, our village was visited by springtime. In early April, the black earth began to appear here and there. With it came the pale green shoots of the butterbur. The sun warmed our hearts and made us feel light and free. By late April, except for some patches persisting in thickest shade, all snow had melted. Fresh greenery budded on the mountainsides and in the fields. There were udo, bracken, and fern tops to be plucked and eaten. I loved to loiter a little on the way to and from school, treading the black earth and picking fresh greens.

After the elation of springtime and promotion in school, summertime came, and we moved into the busiest season of the year. We had to pluck mulberry leaves to feed our silkworms. Before we knew it, time had come to plant rice seedlings in the fields where they would grow till harvest. The fields had to be plowed. I often helped guide the ox in this work. Then the seedlings were taken from their beds and carried in baskets to the paddy fields to be transplanted.

During summer vacation, we weeded the paddies and sweet-potato fields. This was strenuous work under the blazing sun. The worst part was the aching back that came from bending over all day. We had to store grass for fodder in winter. The grown-ups dried it in the fields, and we children hauled it to the storehouse in bundles on our backs. It scratched our necks as we walked along.

I remember we were once made to strip bark from mulberry trees for use—we were told—in making Western-style clothing. How this was to be done remains a mystery to me.

In my fourth and fifth years of primary school, we swam a great deal. The name of the school, Oike, means big pond, but the body of water from which the name derives was in fact no more than three hundred meters around. Still, we enjoyed swimming there—in our undershorts; none of us owned bathing suits—until one year an older student got ensnared in lotus and water lilies and drowned. Thereafter, swimming in Oike pond was forbidden, and we children went to mother's home village, Karusawa, to splash in a small river.

Summer held other pleasures too. After the second weeding of the fields, adults and children took time out in what was called field rest, when there was no work to be done. On the seventeenth of July, in the town of Yokkamachi (it has been incorporated into Tokamachi), the farmers held a horse race in which they rode their work animals. A white horse once won the race two years in a row and seemed certain to win it the third but suddenly—to my immense sadness—dropped dead in midcourse.

The Suwa Shrine festival took place on August twenty-seventh. The major event in all Shinto festivals is the procession in which the divinity is carried through the streets in a massive, richly decorated palanquin (*o-mikoshi*) on the shoulders of men in festive—if sometimes very scanty—attire. The Suwa Shrine festival each year gave us our only chance to see *o-mikoshi* in Suganuma. At the time I am describing, I was too small to take part in the palanquin procession and contented myself with sucking on flavored ice and following my boisterous older cousins about with envious looks.

In autumn, as winter waited just around the corner, the mountains and valleys were made brilliant by scarlet maples and lacquer trees and golden ginkgo, zelkova, and larch. The children's greatest pleasure in this season was searching for chestnuts, gleaming brown through splits in their prickly jackets, or for the sweet purple fruit of the *akebi*. There were the purple-black wild grapes and the berries of the harvest-time silverberry, whose sweet-sour tang I still vividly recall.

When the rice was harvested and the final task of digging sweet potatoes finished, children's chores were done. We were free to play. By this time, not only Kinjiro but Hiroshi as well was old enough to romp mischievously through hills and fields with the other village children.

Thinking back on our experiences, I realize that we were fortunate to have spent our childhoods in the country. Direct physical knowledge of the changing of the seasons and opportunity to see and participate in rural observances helped make up for the sadness of isolation. City people today are in danger of losing part of their humanity in the process of becoming overcivilized. It is a good thing to feel spring's gentleness in the caress of breezes on the skin, to stand in the soft wetness of the rainy season, or to work in the paddy fields protected from the downpour by hat and raincoat of straw. We had our hard times, but being away from the city because of the war and because of father's divine instructions brought us face to face with humankind's impotence in relation to the power and providence of nature. It taught us the precious value of living with nature and helped us understand what it means to be truly human.

SURROGATE CORRESPONDENT

By my fourth and fifth years in primary school, I had already become thoroughly accustomed to life in Suganuma. The biggest local boy in my own class, I was second biggest including boys from Oike too. I began playing baseball and found myself completely accepted by my fellow students. No one was a better pitcher than I was.

In 1950, when the war had been over for five years, I was ready for middle school. But we were still not permitted to return to Tokyo. I was enrolled in what was called the Tokamachi Municipal Middle

School, Oike Branch. It was located on the same site as the Oike Primary School and was attended by students from Suganuma and the nearby villages of Akakura and Tsuike.

My classmates were more numerous then, and I began to think about things more seriously. My emotional and mental life took on new complications. First, there was my pale, first love. The girl was two years behind me in school and excellent at sports and studies. In the schoolyard, my eyes sought her out first of all. Even alone, I blushed to think about her. But the affair went no farther than that. Still, I cherish it as an unforgettable childhood memory.

At about this time, I began to entertain doubts about father. When still small, I neither missed him nor regretted his absence. Later, however, when grown-ups teased me about being fatherless or told me strange stories, I denied everything outwardly but could not suppress inner doubts.

I heard rumors that father was a great religious leader and that Rissho Kosei-kai, which he headed, had nearly fifty branches. All of this made a great impression on the country people. But I took no pride in it. On the contrary, if anything, I was embarrassed at not being like the other children.

My young mind must have noticed that not all children showed unmitigated respect for their fathers. And, with that sensitivity peculiar to the young, I may have perceived that my father was not the object of total admiration at this time either. Mother's family took a very dim view of him and his actions. Her relatives held six family conferences to urge her to divorce the man who had abandoned her and her children for ten years. At the time of one such conference, I was hospitalized in Tokamachi with suspected dysentery. Kinjiro was limping from a skiing accident, and mother had a festering swelling on one leg. She read the Lotus Sutra and chanted the invocation "Hail to the Sutra of the Lotus Flower of the Wonderful Law" diligently for all of us. It is strange that whenever her family began insisting she leave father some kind of sickness or injury developed among us.

In my third, and last, year of middle school, quite naturally, the question of whether I should go to high school in Tokamachi arose. For a solution to the problem, I turned to my teacher, the gentle, kindly Tokuji Watanabe, who had urged me to have more ambition when I said my hope in life was to become a white-collar worker on a regular salary so that I could give mother money. Mr. Watanabe had fallen silent at my comment, though he looked as if he wanted to say something.

In more recent years, I learned that throughout this period, father frequently corresponded with Mr. Watanabe. In November 1977, I visited him in Tokamachi to read the letters exchanged between the two of them. Although no longer teaching, he was in excellent health and, delighted to see me, put in my hands a paulownia-wood box in which he had stored fourteen of the probably many more letters he had received from father. When I asked why he had kept them, he said, "I thought it was splendid that a father should write me so often, all the way from Tokyo. Many of my students' parents never even knew my name."

After I read the letters and learned from them that father had not totally abandoned us but, as strong-willed as he is, had suffered for us mentally, I was moved to tears. I do not know when he found time in his busy schedule to write them. But I am deeply touched to think that late some nights, after a hard day's work, he sat at his desk, grinding ink on an ink stone in preparation to composing them.

One of the letters was written in the summer of my third year in middle school, at a time when I was trying to decide whether to enter high school or go to work at once, as all my classmates intended to do. I had no father to discuss the problem with, and mother was too busy. We had no money. As the oldest son I was tradition-bound to provide for the others. But Mr. Watanabe counseled me to continue my education. Though ultimately I was the only one in my class to do so, he went so far as to buy me a coaching book for the required achievement tests.

From the letters I learned that Mr. Watanabe had journeyed to Tokyo to discuss the issue with father and, in addition, had written him on the subject.

The letter in question was father's reply. In it, he said that my own wishes in relation to my education should take first place in our considerations and asked for Mr. Watanabe's further advice.

In a later letter, he said that he hoped our family situation would be settled by my graduation from high school but that for a while the demands of his religious training forced him to rely on Mr. Watanabe. Having already decided to continue school, I was studying with my teacher in preparation. I would be unable to support mother and my brothers and sisters for a while. Furthermore, chances for good jobs were scarce in Tokamachi, and I wanted to have enough education to get a good job somewhere bigger.

At a still later stage, Mr. Watanabe suggested to father that I study either agriculture or medicine. In one of his letters, father expressed the opinion that this was an excellent idea, since such work would entail study in keeping with the laws of nature and that, fortunately, my efforts in that direction would probably earn the protection of the gods and buddhas. He added, however, that learning alone is insufficient. He advised that I get as much suitable education as I thought fitting, but no more, saying that the most important thing was for me to be diligent in my studies.

In another letter, father thanked Mr. Watanabe for looking out not only for me but also for my two younger brothers. He requested him to urge us to study hard so that one day we could become men of religion capable of leading many people.

At graduation from middle school, in keeping with custom, we took a class trip, to Tokyo. Mr. Watanabe, who went with us, took me to see father. Standing at Uncle Rinzo's side, in front of the old Kosei-kai headquarters, I saw father and Myoko Sensei approaching. My heart was pounding as if this were my first encounter with father. Like a true country bumpkin, I did not even know how to greet him. I remember my anxiety but have no clear recollection of what he said to me or how I answered. That night, instead of returning to the place where my classmates were staying, I spent the night at Myoko Sensei's residence.

Though it may seem odd, in spite of the excitement of meeting father and visiting Kosei-kai headquarters, the thing that made me happiest about the trip to Tokyo was eating white rice, a treat we in the country practically never enjoyed.

Mr. Watanabe says that I was a serious, devoted student. But I remember having no love of study. I worked at it out of a sense of obligation. The same thing was true of morning and evening devotional services. I went through them without enthusiasm simply because my uncle said that if I failed to do so I would not pass my high school entrance examinations. When time for the tests came, I did read the Lotus Sutra more earnestly and, fortunately, passed the examinations for Tokamachi High School, which had a fairly high standard because it was operated by the prefectural government. Throughout this phase of my life, the one person who had my total respect and gratitude was Mr. Watanabe. I still appreciate his help, his correspondence with father, and his kindness in saving the letters and showing them to me. I should like to take this opportunity to thank him once again from the bottom of my heart.

Immediately after visiting Mr. Watanabe and reading father's letters, in 1977, I went to Suganuma to see the school where I had spent nine years—six in primary and three in middle school. At the very moment of my arrival, a huge crane assembly was razing the middle-school building. Had I come two or three days later, it would no longer have been standing. As I watched it being destroyed, faces of classmates and teachers, happy times, and sad times flashed through my mind.

I was of course thrilled at the chance to go to high school. In warm weather, I rode my bicycle the six kilometers to and from school daily. But when winter made this impossible, I shared a room with my elder sister Yoshiko, who was rooming above a tatami dealer in Tokamachi to attend the local girls' school. Yoshiko had helped Kinjiro and me with our studies since we were small. Whenever we ran across an unfamiliar Chinese ideogram in our reading material, we jotted it down and later had her explain it to us. Finally, she convinced us it would be better to look them up in a dictionary and taught us the somewhat complicated process by means of which this is done. She instilled in me the habit of going to a dictionary often—a habit that persists with me still.

The summer after my winter rooming together with Yoshiko, my uncle took me to Tokyo for a second visit. This time, Kinjiro and our youngest brother, Hiroshi, went too. The journey turned out to be preparation for our move back to the city the following year. During it, our uncle was unusually gentle and kind. He bought us sweet rolls and tangerines on the train and took us to a noodle shop in Tokamachi. This was a very exciting experience, since none of us had ever eaten in a restaurant before.

On our first night at the Kosei-kai headquarters, we stayed at Myoko Sensei's, in the room where she kept her family altar. She gave us each a thousand yen spending money—in fresh, crisp bills. None of us had any idea what to do with such an unheard-of sum, and we ended up entrusting it to our uncle.

In an inner room, we knelt in the formal position, bowed, and thereafter remained silent as father spoke. Once again, I do not remember clearly what he said. I recall only our tension and excitement and the additional thousand yen spending money he gave each of us. Kinjiro, Hiroshi, and I went to bed in the room where the devotional altar was but were too excited to get a wink of sleep.

The following day we went to my father's house

in Asagaya. My first impression of it was of an old building with immense corridors. As far as the eye could see, fields and groves spread out around it. There were no neighboring houses. At night we could hear the trains of the Seibu-Shinjuku Line in the distance. At the time, none of us ever dreamed we would come to live in this house, where father kept a large German shepherd dog.

My Suganuma period was drawing to a close, my precious period of boyhood and early youth. Our life in the country immediately before our return to the city was far from comfortable. Still, brought up in a simple, direct relation with the world of nature, among reticent, but warm, relatives and fellow villagers, we had been happy. As I said at the opening of this book, at New Year, 1980, my aunt Nao died. Her husband, my uncle Teizo, who is now seventy-nine—my stubborn, stern uncle, who always insisted that we share all food, no matter how small its quantity—will probably be very lonely without her. Still, in my mind, both of them remain as they were when, as a small child, I first came to live under their roof. Mother has told us all countless times that we are alive today thanks to Uncle Teizo.

PART TWO
TO THE CITY

BACK TO TOKYO

At the beginning of 1954, when the war had been over nine years, some of our family returned to Tokyo. Frankly, I was not overjoyed at the idea. Of course, the new world opening up before me was exciting, but my insecurity was great. First of all, I was going to live with a father with whom I had very unusual relations. When I got ready to leave, Uncle Teizo cautioned me not to think I was returning to the arms of a parent and instructed me to call father nothing but Kaicho Sensei ("President-teacher," the term by which members of Kosei-kai address my father). To make matters more difficult, mother and Hiroshi were to remain in Suganuma for a while; only Kinjiro and I were returning.

My feelings were decidedly mixed. The people with whom I had lived for ten years were closest to me. My uncle and aunt were saddened to see us go. On learning of the day of our departure, my aunt's elderly mother continually said, "So you're leaving us. So you're leaving us," and cried day in, day out.

Out of consideration for auspicious and inauspicious directions, our departures were staggered. Kinjiro left first, on January 18. My sisters and I went with him as far as Tokamachi. To be on time for the first train, we had to leave Suganuma before daylight. At first, Kinjiro put on a bold face and called out that he was going but would be back. Gradually, however, he lost courage and, when the train finally pulled out, waved but looked forlorn enough to cry.

I left on February 8. Once again, I was cautioned against acting as if I were going home and reminded that I was going to stay with Kaicho Sensei. Things turned out exactly as this warning suggested. Father lived upstairs. We lived downstairs. We ate our meals separately and were with him only at morning and evening devotional services. My father's cousins Mr. and Mrs. Takashi Niwano were in charge of the house. Perhaps more surprising than these arrangements, however, was Kinjiro's changed attitude from the moment I arrived. First of all, contrary to our country system of different, less elegant appellations, he immediately began calling me *o-niisan* (elder brother) and acting as if his seniority in the Tokyo house gave him special rank plus the duty of instructing me on all phases of city life. I was amazed at his adaptability and practicality.

At devotionals, our only time with him, father took the opportunity to correct us on various points.

"You were late to devotionals today. Try to do better in the future." He was not severe but spoke to us in an admonishing way that had greater effect than scolding. Sometimes, when a sixth sense told us we were due for correction, Kinjiro and I dashed away after devotionals as fast as possible.

But, even as we ran, we were determined to try to do better from then on. The very sight of our father from the back made us regretful and caused us to reflect on our actions. He has a strange power to produce the effect of a verbal statement even when he has said nothing. His strength is that of a person actually practicing the Buddha's Law. Without speaking, he teaches. It is awe-inspiring. There are people whose very presence clarifies their companions' minds, who make one aware of one's shortcomings without saying a word. My father is such a person. Our relations were, however, of a kind that is difficult for other people to comprehend. Morning greetings were the only words we exchanged. Though the title stuck in our throats, we were supposed to call him Kaicho Sensei, never father. There was no order of precedence for the bath in our house as there often is in traditional Japanese homes. But if Kinjiro and I went in first and father entered later, we quickly rose from the tub and left. Children frequently bathe with parents in Japan, but Kinjiro and I had not done so since we were small children.

We respected father from a distance. But each time we were called upstairs, for a fleeting moment, our blood ties made themselves felt in our minds and we were happy for a chance to be at his side, though when we reached his room we always found him the same stern, awesome man.

MOTHER'S SOLE SUPPORT

Trouble started when mother joined us, bringing Hiroshi with her. He had not seen Tokyo since he was a toddler but was now in the fifth year of primary school. We children actually saw nothing odd in letting Mr. and Mrs. Takashi Niwano run the domestic affairs. But mother saw things differently. Though she was the wife of the house, everything from cooking to financial management was taken out of her hands. She had nothing to do. She was not even allowed to help serve father his meals upstairs. This too was left to Mr. and Mrs. Niwano. Mother ate downstairs with us.

Though a straightforward person who never held a grudge, mother was strong. She was no loser. This trait enabled her to survive the trials of the decade in the country. But coming back to the city to share a roof with her husband and children and finding herself deprived of a wife's place and forced to live as if still separated must have been even harder than isolation in Suganuma.

One day I heard mother and father arguing. She was especially vehement. I had an inkling of what the quarrel must be about. Mother is an impulsive person—this partly accounts for her reputation for resembling the Buddha's wicked, rebellious cousin Devadatta. After the argument, she was sent back to Suganuma for several months.

In his heart, father must have suffered too. In his autobiography, he says, "Even after the ten years of separation were ended, we did not return to normal family life. For another three years we were allowed to share the same roof but not as man and wife and father and children. Perhaps this period was more difficult for us than the ten preceding years."

Mother was violent in a quarrel, but she never said anything spiteful or resentful about father and Myoko Sensei behind their backs. I suspect she was silently proud of her role—even if it was always backstage—in the founding of Rissho Kosei-kai.

But her mainstay throughout everything was the Lotus Sutra. In the days when Kosei-kai was being formed, members were passionately enthusiastic about the sutra and were deeply resolved never to abandon it. No matter how many uncomplimentary things were said about her, mother too always clung to the sutra, her fortress during the hard times in the country and the decade of being abandoned by her husband. Later she told me, "I knew that as long as I persevered in faith in the Lotus Sutra I would never be parted from your father."

In the earliest period of Rissho Kosei-kai's existence we were extremely poor. No doubt mother often showed father by word and deed that she wished he would devote more attention to his family. This is only natural in a wife. But the difficulty is this: such natural behavior is out of place in the home of a religious leader. It is precisely because she behaved in what could be considered a natural wifely fashion that people accused her of hindering father's religious training. Kosei-kai was destined to become an immense organization. It could not allow the wife of its supervising member to make the kind of demands any ordinary wife is entitled to make.

The world of religion transcends ordinary mortal common sense. The family of a religious leader becomes worthy of its standing by accepting sacrifice and even abandonment. The Buddha left his family, but all of its members attained greater happiness than ordinary domestic establishments can know. His father Suddhodana, his aunt and foster mother Mahaprajapati, his wife Yashodara, and his son Rahula all found salvation. I have heard that many officers of Rissho Kosei-kai made sacrifices in those early days very much as my father did.

Mother was victimized, but she did not let her sorrow defeat her. Instead she has attained the happiness she knows now because she never gave up her faith in the Lotus Sutra. The whole time we lived in the country, she got up each morning at three to read from the Threefold Lotus Sutra. We children slept on. At daybreak, she began helping with household chores then, after seeing to our needs, walked three kilometers to the fields for a day's work there.

Raised in the country, mother was strong. The hard work did not get her down. As a matter of fact, she seemed happier in the fields, where labor let her forget her other hardships. Among her greatest psychological burdens were being without a home of her own and being regarded with suspicion by the villagers who would not permit her to attend various gatherings or participate in trips to town.

At night she mended our clothes. If we caught cold, she took ritual baths in icy water at the well and read the sutra for our recovery. When Kinjiro suffered stomachaches and medicine had no effect, she knelt in front of the family altar and prayed to Kaicho Sensei and Myoko Sensei for his recovery. And, as if by miracle, shortly after these prayers Kinjiro usually fell into a peaceful sleep. She later told us that the Threefold Lotus Sutra was her sole support in those times. She was our sole support. I do not remember who wrote it, but I am deeply touched by the poem that says, "A hundred million people have a hundred million mothers, but there's no mother like mine."

I have learned much of great value from father. Mother has taught me much too, and among her lessons the most important is to cling to the Lotus Sutra, no matter what happens.

DEFIANCE

That is the way I feel now. But at sixteen and seventeen I was incapable of such reasoning. Unable to understand why, after ten years' separation, mother and father and we children had to lead an abnormal life under the same roof, I gradually grew more irritated. I knew it was futile to ask for an explanation from father or the people around him. The air was charged with their assurance that our condition was inevitable. I did not really ask even myself for a reason. All my days were spent in irresolute, vague awareness that something was wrong.

A few days after our return to Tokyo I was enrolled in Nihon University High School, located fifteen minutes' walk from father's house. I felt no inferiority about my abilities at schoolwork. But all my city classmates wore their hair long, looked smart, and acted with bright self-assurance. With my hair cropped very short and a strong country accent, I hesitated to start conversations with anyone and for that reason found it hard to fit in. Unlike most other classes, though it had a few good students, ours was a motley group with a large number of indifferent students and problem cases. But they were not the reason for my social failure. My own introverted personality was at fault.

I admired one of my classmates inordinately. He was an excellent student and an extrovert. On our graduation trip, when he asked the pretty guide on our chartered bus for her address, I thought, "You think you're really something, don't you?" and envied him wholeheartedly. I knew, however, that I could never be like him.

I came out a little in my third year. A teacher held English-language study meetings at his home for a few of us each week. Through the study group, I became friends with a boy from Hokkaido. Though this was an excellent chance to get to know other students, I must admit that the greatest attraction of the gatherings was the presence of two pretty, intelligent girl students. Still, the English study group stimulated me to work harder and make better grades than I had been doing for a while.

Nonetheless, I never felt really at home with my classmates and skipped school often. This too may have been a reaction against father. When he or mother asked me why I was not in class, my own confusion and complicated emotions made clear explanation impossible. Once father aggravated my antagonism by telling me to talk straight and stop acting like a sissy.

Perhaps as a vent for my emotions, at about this time, I started having frequent fights with my brother Kinjiro. The causes were always insignificant. The important thing was to fling myself on him and scuffle wildly. The noise often made father summon mother upstairs for a reprimand. Sometimes, after devotionals, he would speak to us himself.

Kinjiro too was defying father and fought often,

not only with me but with others too. At the first sign of a scuffle, he ran to the kitchen to grab a heavy knife, which he then brandished to frighten—certainly not to harm—people. And people tended to get out of his way. Disarming him was my responsibility. Without the least fear, I would walk up to him and take the knife away. On these occasions —if on no others—he put up no resistance. It was as if he had been drained of venom.

During his first year in high school, after being scolded for a brawl with me, Kinjiro actually turned on father. He describes the instance in the following way: "The fight started when I picked my nose, rolled the snot up in balls, and threw them at Koichi. We started battling in the kitchen, and father came downstairs at once—I suspect because Uncle Rinzo told him he ought to bawl us out and let us see, for once, who was boss.

"Father came up to me, shouted an insulting remark, grabbed me by the collar, and smacked me twice with his big hands. The blows made me see stars. I screamed, 'Who do you think you are, hitting me? You're no kind of a father! I'm no son of yours,' and then I leaped on him, hitting him as hard as I could.

"Of course, I didn't have a chance. He was a strong, trained judo man. He struck me once then used some judo technique—*harai-goshi,* or something—to knock me down and rub my head against the floorboards. Uncle Rinzo shouted names at me for striking my father and pinned my legs down. But I kicked him off with all my might and sent him reeling a couple of meters.

"That was the end of the fight. Then father sat me down and started giving me a good talking to.

"'I'm not demanding that you boys be something special. I don't ask you to discipline yourselves in a special way. All you have to be is ordinary human beings. But you must always act with the kind of respect befitting people who partake of the Buddha's food. You must go through morning and evening devotionals properly. If you don't know how, copy what I do. But, whatever you do, you must remember that we partake of the Buddha's food. If you think this is asking too much and that you can't do what I say, I can always disown you.'

"Though I was unreconciled, I kept silent because I realized I should not have turned on my parent. I intended to run away from home and cried all night.

"Being fed by the Buddha's food refers to partaking of offerings after rituals are over and the food has been taken from the altar. Being worthy of such food is a matter of great importance. As I look back on it now, I realize that father's admonition was extremely grave and solemn.

"The real reasons for my turning on him were two. First, although he would not so much as eat with us, he started acting paternal the minute something like my fight with Koichi took place. Second, he was always correcting me and never said a word to Koichi. Both of these things made me so angry that I blew up.

"But, oddly enough, as time went by, the feel of father's body when I leaped on him took root in my mind as a warming memory. Until then, I had never touched him—never, at any rate, since early childhood. Since I had been old enough to know anything at all, he had been distant. But clashing with him physically created a bittersweet, fond recollection: 'How strong my dad is! How smooth my dad's skin is!' This was the first time I ever felt that I was bound to him with blood ties, the first time these hands ever touched a man I could call father."

I never had a chance like Kinjiro's. When we had fights, it was always Kinjiro that father scolded or struck. He never laid a hand on me. Something kept us from touching hands or hearts. I remained unable to find an outlet for my pent-up emotions.

Shortly after Kinjiro's rebellion, a major event occurred in our house. The Niwanos moved to a place of their own, and father began eating his meals with us. I later learned that father and Myoko Sensei had discussed the matter and had decided to end both father's discipline period of living apart from his family and mother's thirteen years of hardship. In the preface to an earlier book of mine entitled *Kokoro no naka no Sampomichi* (A Path in My Heart), mother describes her own state of mind at that time: "Then I came to understand with my whole being the depth of a woman's karma. In my own way, I understood

the profundity of spiritual guidance and of the
Buddha Way. But many doubtful points remained
unresolved in my mind. When I thought about them,
I seemed to lose my bearings. The president of Kosei-
kai, who should have been my mentor, was close at
hand. This should have made being taught easy. But
I was not permitted to speak to him. Consequently,
I had to resolve my doubts myself, the best way I
could. My sole teacher was the Threefold Lotus
Sutra. It was all I had to rely on.

"Day after day, after staying up late at night looking after the children, I got up at three in the morning
to read the sutra quietly in front of the family altar.
The same kind of days continued for three years
after our return to Tokyo. During that time, I discovered that all the sufferings of this world arise
from within us ourselves. When I knew this, all the
perplexity and pain that had lurked in my mind
vanished. And, as if my awareness had been awaited,
our period of living in separation, though under one
roof, ended. We were a family again."

I believe that, realizing mother's change of heart,
Myoko Sensei commented on her long years of suffering and suggested that father open his heart to his
wife and live with her again.

But long habits are not obliterated on short notice.
Our meals together were no warm family gatherings.
Father talked on many topics. Mother and we children listened silently. I was especially tightly shut up
in my own shell.

As was the general rule, upon graduating from Nihon University High School, I took entrance examinations for Nihon University. Father congratulated me when I told him I had passed them.

I entered the Japanese Literature Department. But soon college lost its appeal. I had thought the university was a place where students worked hard. I was disillusioned to find that this is not true. Once again, my introversion prevented my improving my way of life by making friends in sports, haunting the coffee shops as other students did, or playing mah-jong. In about the middle of my first year, I stopped attending classes regularly. Sometimes I stayed home reading two or three days in a row. Sometimes I pretended to go to class and then did nothing but wander around the streets of the Kanda district, where the campus was located. Browsing in the Kanda secondhand-book stores was my only, mild, pleasure in a long string of gray days.

HOPING FOR
SOMEONE TO SCOLD ME

When I was a second-year high-school student, father instructed me to start training in Japanese fencing (kendo). He selected a nearby training hall called Taigi-juku because he admired the courtesy and good posture of the trainees there and liked the way they looked directly into the eyes of the person they conversed with. Feeling a little guilty about skipping classes often and slightly interested in kendo, I followed his instructions. On the day I signed up, my father's cousin Takashi accompanied me to the hall. The following New Year, father wrote Tokuji Watanabe, my primary-school teacher in Suganuma, to tell him of my new endeavor in hope of setting his mind to rest about me.

The head of the Taigi-juku, Tokichi Nakamura, was an illustrious kendo expert. His son Taro won first place in the All Japan Kendo Championship Tournament in 1955, his first time to participate in it. In 1957 and 1958, he took second place and then, in 1959, took first place again. Many of the most famous kendo men of the twentieth century attended the Nakamuras' school.

Tokichi Nakamura was a strict, kindly man who taught us the courtesies and techniques of fencing sternly but with intimate warmth. Our practice sessions took place at seven every evening except Friday and Sunday. Friday was free, and on Sunday training started at nine in the morning. After a student reached the level of first *dan,* he was required to attend only three practice sessions weekly. The training was so stimulating and encouraging that, when a junior in college, I requested the master of the school to permit me to be a live-in trainee for the two months of summer vacation. He granted my request.

A young man who had come up from Kyushu and

I were the two live-in trainees. Since it got light very early, we arose at five each morning and began our day by cleaning toilets, corridors, and training hall. When this was done, the master of the school joined us for morning workout. Our afternoons were consumed with various chores and errands. At night, large groups of students came for practice. We worked with all of them and then remained up, no matter how late, until all guests had gone home. The heavy schedule and summer heat soon got us down. Ten days, then twenty, and finally one month passed. Suddenly, one morning, without saying anything, I went home. The following morning the master stood in our entryway and, in a voice audible throughout the house, shouted, "What's the idea of running away? You were the one who wanted to train with me for two whole months. I agreed to look after you for two months. You're like one of our family. Come on! You're going back with me!"

I was taken back to training school. That evening, after workout, I got a good lecturing. Of everything said to me then, I remember the following statement about truthfulness most: "One lie costs you the ten years it takes to regain people's trust." This warning is still one of my guidelines.

I was very much frightened of Tokichi Nakamura the day he came to bring me back to school. But, at the same time, I was happy that he cared enough to scold me. I must have been looking for someone who would do just that.

Some time after I reached the grade of third *dan,* Tokichi Nakamura fell ill. In 1969, at the early age of forty-seven, Taro Nakamura died of stomach cancer. Two years later, Tokichi Nakamura died at the age of eighty-five. His son's death was concealed from him until the last. With his passing, my own kendo career came to an end, except for the two or three bouts I have a year with young students at Kosei-kai's martial-arts training hall.

FATHER'S TEARS

Mother was very disturbed that I cut classes in college often and that I showed no interest in school-work. Father knew what I was doing and scolded mother for it. This made me angry. Why did he take it out on her? On days when he reprimanded mother, I stayed in bed and refused to attend family morning devotionals. Later, feeling that I ought to go, I would take briefcase in hand and leave the house, though I practically never went to school. Instead I headed for the bookshops of the Kanda Jimbo-cho district. Though I admit I have one of the worst senses of direction in Japan, I know that part of Tokyo very well. I bought and enjoyed many books there—the novels of Soseki Natsume were great favorites. Wandering through the bookstores or reading in my room, I often wondered why I had been born into a home where the father could abandon his family for ten years and, even after rejoining them, insist that the children call him Kaicho Sensei and remain upstairs, refusing even to eat with us.

One morning after devotionals, father said he had something to tell me. Mother stayed behind too. "Right now," he began, "your duty is to go to school and study. I don't know what's happened to you or what's on your mind. But cutting class and lounging around the house all the time mean you're refusing to play the part assigned to you. Each person has a place to be and something to do. It's important to fulfill one's tasks as well as possible. You see that, don't you?"

I looked into his face and saw tears in his eyes. For the first time in my life, I saw father cry. His scolding aroused no resentment in me. Instead I felt refreshed by it. His tears showed that there was a true parent-child bond between us.

Not long afterward, father asked what I thought of the idea of leaving Nihon University and transferring to the Faculty of Buddhism at Rissho University. Eager for any change that would shake me out of my rut, I agreed but selected the Faculty of English Literature, not Buddhism. I was interested in English literature and still disinclined to become a professional specialist in religion.

Secretly I dreamed of escaping the oppressive atmosphere of home, emigrating to Brazil, and making a way for myself in a new land. But, finally, when I admitted to myself that this could never be,

I changed to the Faculty of Buddhism and settled down in the place where I was supposed to settle down. This was less a transfer in curriculum than a fresh start from the status of freshman.

Fortunately, I came into contact with a teacher for whom I could feel great respect in the person of the late Yukio Sakamoto. Although he suffered from cataracts that greatly reduced his vision, he went on studying and even headed the Institute for the Comprehensive Study of the Lotus Sutra. He showed me that being a scholar and a truly fine human being demand warmth and indomitable spirit.

I remember with great clarity the following words he spoke during a lecture: "The universe is sustained by a great harmony. We are part of that harmony and live because of it. You sit studying now in a classroom. But if the harmony of the universe were broken and if earth were to collide with some other planet, you, the classroom, and I would all cease to exist."

For me this was a powerfully impressive first inkling of the startling wonder and mystery of the operation of the cosmos. Though I cut other classes regularly, I attended Professor Sakamoto's with fair faithfulness.

My academic career was of unusual length. Counting the time I spent in Nihon University and at Rissho University too, my undergraduate education lasted nine years, largely because of poor class attendance. I was still unsettled and rebellious and still unwilling to go to school as I should. Even when I entered graduate school, I had not actually completed my undergraduate work. But Professor Sakamoto said I was qualified and urged me to go ahead, since he felt academic background is important to people with influence in society and public affairs.

Once again, in graduate school, I took longer than other people because I would not attend class. Whereas most people finish their master's degree in two years, I took three. I graduated from high school in 1956 and left graduate school in 1968, twelve years later. If I did not go to class often, I did read a great deal. And my reading has stood me in good stead.

FOUR DAYS' FLIGHT

The complications of home and school upset me tremendously. To make matters worse, around 1960 the Kosei-kai committee responsible for such matters at last decided that I should be designated father's official successor. Though I had suspected this was in the offing, when the blow came I lost all remnant of interest in schoolwork.

Before this, at major Kosei-kai events, father had instructed me to sit on the platform with him. I disliked the idea of being displayed as the president's son. Father was an important figure, but I had done nothing for the organization or its believer-members.

I was a mere student with absolutely no knowledge of the world or experience in spreading the religious teachings of the group. It seemed wrong to select such a person as me to be successor to father on the strength of nothing more than family ties. The idea terrified me, and I could not bring myself to consent to it. The little pride and self-respect I had could not tolerate exposure to the public eye as heir to a position that many other faithful, experienced members of the organization were better qualified to fill.

Still, when I realized how puny my own pride and self-respect were in the face of the consensus of the organization's leaders and the will of the president, I was crushed under an oppressive weight and could not sleep nights. No amount of weeping and wailing would do any good. Gradually a complex emotion transcending fear alone grew in intensity till I could no longer bear to be at home with other members of the family. I wanted to run away to some distant place.

Then, leaving a note saying, "I'll be back in two or three days," on mother's dressing table, I went out the front door. An autumn rain was falling. At Tokyo Station, I bought a ticket for Nishi Kago-shima, at the southern end of the southern island of Kyushu, about fifteen hundred kilometers away. This was the first time I had traveled alone so far from home. My intention was to give myself a

that touched me: "I didn't choose to become president. It was just in the natural flow of things. I went along with the flow and accepted the decision of the others. I am able to work hard and do my best because of the tremendous support the leaders and other members give me."

Then I saw what I had to do. I must not try to run counter to the natural current of things. The time had come for me to open my eyes to the great harmony of the world and to my own part in it.

PART THREE

TO A NEW BEGINNING

ON BEING A BEGINNER

In May 1964, I was overjoyed at the chance to play a game of golf with father. It was the first time I had engaged in any kind of amusement with him since that trip years ago to the hot spring (and that had been fundamentally therapeutic to cure my brother Kinjiro's rash). The bright, sunny weather matched my mood. I did poorly at first, since I had never played golf before. But driving the ball farther than father thrilled me greatly. I had always assumed I could never do anything as well as he. Self-confidence was beginning to emerge in me. I was breaking out of my shell and becoming less self-involved.

In the past I had considered Rissho Kosei-kai something gloomy and unpleasant. A lecture I attended one day at the education department completely erased this image from my mind and showed me that Kosei-kai members offered people teachings that were not only sound, but also refreshing.

On November 14, 1964, mother and father and I

left on a trip to India. It was the first time I had ever traveled with the two of them together, their first trip since their marriage, and my first trip abroad.

India is certainly vast enough to be called a sub-continent. Everything about it—especially the contradictions apparent everywhere—is big. Its population of more than 672 million people speaks well over two hundred languages and dialects. Poverty in this birthland of the world's loftiest spiritual culture, culminating in the philosophy of Shakyamuni Buddha, is crushing. Most of the Indians I saw on my first walk in Calcutta were barefoot. Members of our hotel staff slept, fully clothed, on the lobby floor. One day before dawn, in a train station at Patna, in the north where nights are cold, we saw many people sleeping curled up and huddled together on the floor hoping for a little more warmth than their single white garments could afford. Most of the population suffered from malnutrition and had legs and arms no bigger around than slim bamboo poles. These frail-looking people worked as coolies, carrying heavy loads for pittances, on which they had to live. Nonetheless, far from seeming defeated by their lot, they conversed in voices so loud they seemed to be quarreling.

Of course the many relics and historical sites associated with Buddhism left a deep impression on me. But the most important result of the trip was the effect it had on me personally. The contrasts of India awakened deep within me a new vitality that I did not understand fully then and still do not entirely comprehend. After leaving India, we returned to Japan by way of Colombo, Singapore, Manila, Hawaii, and Los Angeles. When the trip was over, though still not convinced to follow in father's footsteps, I had determined to try to make something meaningful of my life.

GOOD AND BAD HABITS

At New Year, 1968, for the first time, I led readings from the Lotus Sutra at ceremonies in Kosei-kai's Great Sacred Hall. When I mounted the platform, my heart was pounding. The beating grew stronger as I came face to face with the immense statue of Shakyamuni Buddha that is our main focus of devotion. Yet at other times, unaccountably, my heartbeat seemed to drop to a whisper. Obviously I was in an extreme state of anxiety and emotional stress.

After six months or a year of training in this kind of work, I gained a certain amount of composure. I learned that the sole way to bring rectitude and calm to an uneasy mind is to keep the Lotus Sutra, read it, recite it, expound it, and copy it. These practices instill good habits in the mind, and habit is a powerful force, as the nineteenth-century Swiss writer and philosopher Henri Frédéric Amiel points out in his *Journal intime,* where he says habit is more valuable than ideology. According to him, habit is a living ideology incarnate and instinctified. Amiel says that changing an ideology is as easy as changing a title whereas acquiring new habits is as difficult as it is important. "To learn new habits is everything, for it is to reach the substance of life. Life is but a tissue of habits."

Amiel's words are highly significant. Habit is a kind of second nature. We Buddhists must never underrate the importance of acquiring the habits of correct discipline according to correct teachings. The Flower Garland Sutra (*Avatamsaka-sutra*) says that merely hearing many teachings cannot rid the mind of delusions unless it is accompanied by practical action. Repeated practical actions result in habit. My gradually becoming accustomed to leading religious services taught me the immense importance of both habit and practical action.

In other aspects of my relations with Kosei-kai, however, I still had a long way to go. In 1967, I bought a secondhand automobile, learned to drive, and started commuting to headquarters daily. The members got into the habit of calling me "*Waka-sensei*" (young teacher), and I answered when so addressed. But I still lacked the courage to overcome my introversions and to initiate conversations. I did not fit into the lighthearted, free exchanges the other members enjoyed.

As a matter of custom, Kosei-kai members greet one another by bringing their palms together before them in a reverent attitude and bowing slightly. It seemed to me, however, that many people were affording me exaggerated reverence simply because I was the son of the president of the organization. Since it caused me considerable emotional discomfort, I mentioned the subject to my wife. This is what she said: "They are simply expressing their gratitude to the Buddha through you. There is no reason for you to be uncomfortable." I felt much better when I was able to look at the situation in this light. I was still a beginner with much to learn. A beginner reacts with freshness to each novel situation. Prizing this freshness, I resolved then never to forget how it feels to be a beginner and to know the embarrassment being treated worshipfully causes.

Earlier I spoke of the good effects of habit. But habit can have ill effects too. It can dull human awareness. For instance, a person who has been revered and respected by others for a long time comes to take such respect as his natural due. He becomes conceited. He adopts rigid attitudes, and his sensitivity to everything beyond his own limitations of habit atrophies. Just as human eyes and ears cannot perceive light and sound beyond certain limits, so limitations can be set to human emotional sensibilities. For instance, most people sympathize with the victim and condemn the murderer they read about in the newspaper. But these same people react impersonally to thousands, perhaps millions, of deaths reported in coverage of a distant war. War casualties are not people, only statistics. (Any movement for world peace that hopes to succeed must bring people everywhere to realize vividly that each war death is not a number in a column but the lamented extinction of a unique human life.)

Refusing to become habit-atrophied and remembering to view everything with the open eye of the beginner, we must all strive to be sensitive to everything around us. The sensitivity limits of a great person like Shakyamuni Buddha were immense. He shared the suffering of all humankind and all sentient beings everywhere as intensely as if they stood before him. Observing the way he strives to save people and his worldwide activities in the name of peace, I believe that father's sensitivity limits too are very wide. I am sure this kind of expansiveness is the mark of an outstanding person, of a person who is human in the best sense of the word. All of us who are still training in the Buddha Way must strive to become people of this kind.

FASTING

After our return from India, I began looking for a definite way to convince myself to undertake regular attendance at the Kosei-kai headquarters. During my roamings in the bookstore district of Kanda, by accident I happened on a book called *Nishishiki Danjiki-ho* (The Nishishiki Fasting Method); bought it;

read it; and, in May 1965, entered the Nishishiki Health Center, in Ichigaya, Tokyo, for training in fasting.

The first four days were a preliminary period of diet reduction, with smaller and smaller meals provided each day. Then we entered the true eight-day fasting phase. Though permitted to drink water and persimmon tea, we were forbidden all food. The first and second days of fast, I managed fairly well. But, on the third and fourth, I was so hungry that my entire body grew sluggish and painful.

The Nishishiki regimen demanded that morning and evening I descend from my third-floor room in the health center, take hot and cold baths, do certain prescribed calisthenics, and then exercise on a piece of equipment devised by the organization. The climb back up three flights of steps after each session was excruciating. Time and time again I wondered why I had ever started fasting.

But I was mentally fortified to see the course through by having read the health-center book. This forewarned me of the various changes that would occur in my body and thus prevented my worrying about what was happening to me. In addition, I enjoyed the careful guidance of experienced teachers.

Parallels can be drawn between this situation and religion. Ultimately religion must be experienced, but hearing doctrines preached and reading them in books provide minimal knowledge enabling a person to accept religious experience correctly. Few people find enlightenment unaided. Most of us cannot come to salvation this way. Moreover, self-attained, self-styled enlightenment is sometimes dangerous because erroneous. Leaders claiming special access to novel truths can lead their followers along disastrous paths, as was tragically illustrated in 1978 by the mass suicide of the People's Temple group from the United States. My experience with fasting convinced me that the one way to salvation is the correct study of correct teachings and correct discipline under the guidance of outstanding leaders.

When the actual fasting was over, we still had considerable unpleasantness ahead. The gradual increase of food allowed after the fast caused me much suffering, though it was of a kind different from the actual deprivation of meals. During the initial diet-reduction phase, the person is tense about what is going to happen and realizes that a complete cutoff of food is in the offing. After the fast, however, appetite is fierce. Nonetheless, we were permitted to eat only small quantities that were slowly increased day by day. Tolerating this leisurely return to normal diet demanded tremendous psychological effort.

The Nishishiki fasting method claims to purify the alimentary tract and increase digestive efficiency, thus making possible good health on small amounts of food. It further claims to clear the mind and activate psychological operations.

In my own experience, I found that during the fasting phase I required less sleep. I was awake bright and early in the morning and remained alert until late at night. In the post-fast period, when my mind was very clear, I concentrated on reading. As my bodily strength gradually returned, when the worst was over, I began to enjoy the sensation of an empty stomach.

When I passed, totally refreshed, through the health-center door at the end of the full twenty-day course, I felt ready for anything. Having endured the trial of the fast, I was confident that I could overcome other obstacles too. Since then, I have fasted on two occasions, once for four days and once for two.

It is not certain how many times Shakyamuni Buddha fasted during the six years between his departure from his home and his enlightenment. But during his period of ascetic discipline he is thought to have subsisted on one sesame seed and one grain of rice daily and almost to have starved to death. As a consequence of these rigors, however, he discovered that punishing the body does not lead to enlightenment. He then ceased austerities, bathed in the Nairanjana River, accepted rice gruel offered by a maiden from a nearby village, and, physically renewed, once again concentrated on reflection and meditation. (The small amounts of food fed us during the post-fast period renewed our physical strength as the rice-and-milk gruel did that of the Buddha.)

During his youth, when a member of the Tengu Fudo training group, my father underwent two disciplinary diets: one in which he ate no grain of any kind and another in which he ate nothing that had come in contact with fire. In his autobiography, he says he does not consider these trials wasted effort. In another of his books, *Bukkyo no Inochi—Hokekyo* (The Lotus Sutra, Life and Soul of Buddhism), he says, "Supreme enlightenment is seeing and living in accordance with the universe as it truly is. Ascetic practices rejecting the physical body are not wasteful. But they are only one stage. True enlightenment lies beyond them."

STAGE FRIGHT

For all the confidence my fasting experience gave me, I could not overcome my fear of addressing large groups. I found even private conversation with strangers difficult. On January 12, 1964, I was terrified at the idea of having to read a message for my father at a meeting of the western Japan young adults' groups, in Osaka. Father could not attend the meeting. Just back from a trip to Europe in connection with his work for the Peace Delegation of Religious Leaders for Banning Nuclear Weapons, he was confined to bed with a cold. Seeing that I was nervous at the prospect of making a speech, Moto-yuki Naganuma, chief director of Rissho Kosei-kai, suggested that we run through the message two or

three times for practice. Even during those rehears-
als, my heart pounded.

On the next day, when I actually had to take the
platform, I thought my chest would burst with the
hammering of my heart. Oddly enough, however,
when I rose to speak, I was suddenly calm and
managed to get through the speech with fair success,
to my own great relief and to that of the directors.
That night, Director Naganuma and some other
members took me to dinner. I drank more sakè that
night than I had ever drunk at one time in my whole
life.

Now that I reflect on it, I suppose father chose not
to appear on that and other official occasions in order
to give me chances to participate in headquarters
affairs and to come into contact with the directors
and members of the organization. His motive was
sound, but each such occasion caused me torment.
I considered it intolerably bold on my part to pre-
sume to address leaders who had undergone great
religious discipline and members whose knowledge
of life was extensive when I was deficient in both
training and experience. Even today, eighteen years
later, I am still tense and nervous when I must take
the rostrum in front of a group of such people.

After 1964, I participated in more and more official
ceremonies all over the country, though I was still
far from used to it. Gradually, reading father's mes-
sages for him ceased being sufficient: I was required

to deliver speeches of my own. The idea frequently made me so despondent that I could say nothing to anyone. Never a glib person, my ineptness with words, aggravated by nervousness on such occasions, must have caused the branch heads and other leaders much worry and discomfort.

For a week in advance I worked on the text of my first independent speech—or greeting, as it was called—to be delivered in 1968 at the installation of a focus of devotion at a Kosei-kai branch in Chiba Prefecture, not far from Tokyo. When the day came, I fell into such total confusion that I did not know what I was doing. I remember nothing about the ceremony or the reception my message got. But the branch head made a tape recording of my talk. Later I heard it with great satisfaction because I sounded more serious and convincing than I had imagined I could be.

Still, I lacked confidence. Often, just before a speech, I developed fevers, sometimes high enough to force me to remain in bed and cancel the talk. Nonetheless, no matter how I had to force myself to attend them, gatherings like enshrinements of focuses of devotion brought me great merit and purified my own heart by allowing me to observe and share the emotions—sometimes tearful—and joy members feel on such occasions.

In a single year, I must have delivered speeches twenty or thirty times. I cannot remember all my topics, but I do recall once speaking on shrimp. There are several explanations—mostly linguistic—for the use of shrimp as an auspicious accompaniment to such festivals as New Year celebrations and weddings. But I prefer to believe that the shrimp is selected as a symbol of the resilience and pliancy of life, since it periodically sheds its old shell for the sake of growth and development. Like the shrimp, human beings should periodically cast off old shells in order to remain young and vigorous. I remember this speech topic because it pertains strongly to me.

When I first began touring regional chapters to make addresses I was often requested to follow an established Japanese custom by writing a commemorative remark with brush and ink on a special paper-covered square of cardboard made and sold in Japan precisely for that purpose. These squares are covered with white paper on one side and with colored paper flecked with gold or silver foil on the other. Having studied calligraphy only as an elective for one year in high school, I was certainly no skilled artist with the ink brush. Usually, perhaps as a reminder to myself, I wrote the word *shoshin,* or beginner, and selected the foil-flecked side, thinking it was the front, not the back.

Once, to my great embarrassment, someone corrected my error, pointing out that the white side is the right one to use. On the next day, however, Motoyuki Naganuma informed me that, strictly speaking, I had followed proper procedure. Although practically no one abides by it, the truly correct thing is to write calligraphy on the foil-flecked side and to reserve the white side for ink paintings. But, after thinking about the matter, I decided to join everyone else, not to be a stickler for the correct, and to follow general usage by writing on the white side. I imagine Mr. Naganuma does so too.

PILGRIMAGE TO MOUNT SHICHIMEN

On the several occasions in the past when I had heard father talk about pilgrimages to Mount Shichimen and had seen photographs in our albums of him at the head of a group clad in white with bands tied around their heads and with walking staffs in their hands, I had thought that this must be severe training. Father and mother had both recommended that I take part in a similar pilgrimage when the chance arose, and I agreed that it was a good idea.

Mount Shichimen is mentioned (under slightly different appellations) in the writings of Nichiren, the great thirteenth-century Japanese religious leader and founder of the Buddhist sect that bears his name. In the final years of his life, Nichiren lived on a mountain called Minobu. At the top of Mount Shichimen is a Shinto shrine to Shichimen Daimyo-jin, considered the tutelary divinity of the temple Kuon-ji, on Mount Minobu. The shrine is said to have been founded by Nichiro, a disciple of Nichiren. Since March 14, 1947, Rissho Kosei-kai has invoked the name of Shichimen Daimyojin as a deity protecting people who believe in and disseminate the Lotus Sutra in the final age of the Law of Shakyamuni Buddha.*

I had my first chance to make a pilgrimage in July 1968, with a small group including my wife, who had already climbed the mountain once; my nephew; and four other people close to me. As we left home, mother told me to be reverent and pray for protection. The others who saw us off promised to pray for our well-being.

It was pouring rain when we arrived at the town of Minobu the night before our morning climb. The downpour seemed ominous, especially since I had already heard many strange tales about Mount Shichimen. As a consequence of karmic causes and effects, powerful men had been known to collapse on the way. People with evil intentions had been stopped in their tracks, immobilized.

It was still raining the next morning at three, when we arose. After morning devotionals, hoping against hope that the rain would stop at daybreak, we set out by car for Shiraito (white-thread) Falls, where we made final preparations at temple lodgings there.

*The Buddha prophesied that after his death his teaching, or Law, would persist through three ages: one in which it was preserved in its true form, one in which it was preserved in counterfeit form, and one in which it would exist though there would be neither practice of nor enlightenment to it. The age in which we now live is believed to be the final one.

Shiraito Falls too has an interesting story attached to it. For many years, women were forbidden on Mount Shichimen (as they were on many other mountains where Buddhist temples and monasteries were located). Oman, a favorite of Ieyasu, the first Tokugawa shogun, was an ardent believer in the Lotus Sutra. Arguing that forbidding women on Mount Shichimen ran counter to the Lotus Sutra teaching to the effect that women as well as men may attain buddhahood, she first purified her body in the waters of Shiraito Falls then boldly climbed the mountain, violating and thereby removing its taboo against women.

Her act is an example of the spirit of a true believer. No guardian deity would punish a person who reads the Lotus Sutra with his whole physical being and trusts it from the bottom of his heart. By boldly proving this, Oman showed herself to be a brave woman with the strength of her convictions.

When our preparations were finished, chanting "Hail to the Sutra of the Lotus Flower of the Wonderful Law" and beating ritual drums, we started up what is called the front pilgrimage path. The rain continued to pour down on us. At first it distracted my thoughts. But, before I knew it, I had forgotten the weather and was savoring the indescribable happiness of finding myself absorbed in chanting and drum beating.

To ensure that no one lagged behind, we moved

at a fairly slow pace and rested from time to time. At eight o'clock in the morning, we reached the halfway lodgings and stopped for a breakfast that our early exercise made especially delicious.

When we had climbed a little higher, the previously total cloud cover broke, revealing patches of blue sky. The rain had practically stopped, and we all felt refreshed and stronger as we went on chanting and drumming with renewed vigor. The closer we came to the top, the quicker we moved. We reached the summit in about four and a half hours after our start. I was elated to have accomplished the same difficult training my predecessors had carried out. At the same time, I was sobered by the knowledge that people in the past probably had a harder time accomplishing the feat than we.

We rested for about an hour at the top and viewed the main shrine hall before starting our descent by the rear pilgrimage path. At about one-third the way, we stopped for lunch and a rest. Then we continued. But the way seemed very long. No matter how far we walked the bottom was never in view.

Finally, however, we reached the last temple-lodgings stop, where we turned respectfully to the mountain and, with a great sense of relief and fulfillment, chanted "Hail to the Sutra of the Lotus Flower of the Wonderful Law" again to the accompaniment of ritual drumming. As the sound of our voices lingered on the air, I felt as if I had become a person very different from the one who had started the climb that morning. The rain had stopped entirely.

Then I recalled that our children were waiting for us at the lodgings at Minobu. To my remark to this effect, my wife announced that the children had been on her mind for a long time. (Mothers are more attentive to their offspring's needs than fathers are.) Completely engrossed in chanting only a little while earlier, I was being drawn back into the ordinary world.

This pilgrimage was an important experience for me. I still have the drum I carried. It is punctured by my fervent beating during the climb.

LEARNING FROM BELIEVERS

The sincerity of believers is always the most stirring part of Kosei-kai ceremonies. Testimonials of actual experience with the Law strike me especially deeply because, though I have theoretical understanding of the wonderful characteristics of Buddhism and have heard much about the splendid things it can do, my knowledge and understanding are merely intellectual. They have not yet taken full form in flesh and blood. Coming into contact with people who have directly experienced the working of the Law and hearing their voices allow me to feel the blessedness of Buddhism with my whole person. Moreover, by bringing powerfully home the sincerity and purity of believers in the Law, testimonials help me unite with other members, share their emotions, and rejoice and weep with them. Because it moves and purifies the heart, the testimonial is a vital aspect of the Rissho Kosei-kai practice of faith.

In the final analysis, we are all weak human beings with individual sorrows. But, as long as we remain isolated from each other, sorrow can only deepen, and there can be no salvation from it. Fellowship of believers, however, brings help and comfort. Sufferers from the same disease can encourage and comfort one another with advice and shared experiences because they have a common basis of understanding. They can say to each other such things as "Don't worry. There's no danger of a serious attack" or "This new treatment I've been trying really works," and the words carry weight.

Seven years ago I visited Kumamoto and met some Kosei-kai members afflicted with what is called the Minamata disease, a horribly debilitating, sometimes fatal, illness brought on by industrial pollution of the environment. One woman patient, who had only recently become a member, had already lost her father to it. Her mother and husband too had been stricken. Though still young in the organization, she requested the duty of guiding other victims, since she knew and understood their pain. Her eagerness to take the initiative in helping people like herself impressed me with the strength of her faith and of the faith of the whole Kosei-kai and illustrated the way sufferers can effectively help others afflicted with the same suffering.

Alcoholics can help one another better than non-drinkers because they see in the people they try to help a reflection of themselves and find strength in aiding others. All the best advice in the world will not convince a drunkard to abandon the bottle. But concerned help from a person who knows the horrors of the alcoholic's plight can work wonders. Rissho Kosei-kai embodies this truth by insisting that a person seeking salvation must find it by helping save others.

Only humankind can solve the problems facing the world today. The only way for humanity to work out its difficulties is for all of us to share one another's suffering and make the kind of efforts attributed to the bodhisattvas described in the Lotus Sutra as rising from the very earth to save all sentient beings. In the many believers I have observed in Kosei-kai I have seen these bodhisattvas at work. Concern for the well-being and happiness of others is the heart of Buddhist compassion. It is my prayer that as many people as possible will first devote themselves to compassionate action on the personal level and then move to the wider social scale to attempt to remove darkness, shed light, and create a truly brighter society free of the social injustice that allows one sector of the population to victimize all others by polluting the environment that we all must share.

Among many other things, from Kosei-kai believers in many parts of the nation I have learned to reaffirm my own conviction that one must always remember to be a beginner. I have found that leaders and members in outlying rural chapters tend to be astonishingly kind and pure of heart. People in large chapters where official events are common seem to become too accustomed to things and to lose a little of their purity. Perhaps they forget the meaning of being a beginner and of taking a positive, fresh view of their tasks in life.

The Chinese writer of the Ming dynasty Lu Hsin-wu describes the actions of many human beings and, in doing so, provides us with a guideline for what to avoid. "It is the common ill of people of the world to be lazy and muddled before the event, hasty of hand and disorderly of foot during the event, and distracted and slack after the event. All this is to rob the event."

PART FOUR
TO GREATER GROWTH

MYOKO NAGANUMA SENSEI

Mother and father have often told me that Kosei-kai would not exist had it not been for Mrs. Myoko Naganuma, or Myoko Sensei as she was called by all members. From my early years I had my own impressions of this important figure.

Before I began primary school, she was the gentle lady who called me by my nickname Kochan and gave me good things to eat. While I was living in the country apart from father, she was the wicked woman who had broken up our family. After my return to Tokyo, she was a kindly, but sometimes frightening teacher.

My recollections of her are strongest—indeed stronger than my remembrances of father for the same period—for the time immediately prior to our evacuation to the country. It was during this time that she once insisted I be in the front row of a group photograph of Kosei-kai leaders at the old headquarters. I vividly remember the puff of white smoke the magnesium flash made when it went off.

Myoko Sensei often gave me cakes and sweets, but my brother Kinjiro—even then more aggressive than I—got the lion's share and taunted me with it till I chased him and started fights that invariably won a scolding from mother.

I have already mentioned punching a hole in the shoji paper to peep through at her when she accompanied father to Suganuma on one of his three visits to us during our stay there. I have also mentioned receiving a thousand yen from her when I visited her house with my uncle just before we returned to Tokyo for good, in 1954.

Myoko Sensei died three and a half years later, in 1957. During those years I saw her rarely. For one thing I was a high-school student till 1956. Then I started my aimless early college career, when I practically never went to Kosei-kai headquarters. She traveled extensively in the outlying districts and, in her last year, spent quite a long time recuperating from extreme fatigue in a hot-spring resort in Yamanashi Prefecture.

Nonetheless, she sometimes visited our home in Asagaya and usually brought gifts, which she presented with a word about my health and schoolwork. I still have a sword she gave me, and Kinjiro has a Leica camera that was her gift.

Throughout her whole life, Myoko Sensei was a woman of great compassion. Those who knew her had direct experience of her compassionate thought and action and the strengthening effect they had on religious faith. She frequently gave things away. Though the second highest officer in the whole organization, she prepared food for others with her own hands. In the last years of her life, many important construction projects were under way for Kosei-kai—the Second Training Hall, the Great Sacred Hall, and Kosei-gakuen School. Members who devoted time and labor preparing and grading the land for the buildings were lodged in a nearby hall and rose at three or four in the morning to do their part. Myoko Sensei cooked for them and sometimes gave them her own clothing.

She was very frugal in her own way of life. It is said that she deliberately chose light-colored kimono fabrics, the age of which could be concealed by repeated dyeings, each time a darker color. She wore her wooden geta clogs till they were level with the ground then made a reverent gesture and said a word of thanks as she burned them for firewood.

It was her joy to see happiness on the faces of people to whom she unstintingly gave her own possessions. No doubt she accompanied each gift with encouraging remarks. Many of the people I know were recipients of her kindness and treasure the things she gave them.

On the other hand, she could be very severe and stern. She mercilessly pointed out other people's failings. Indeed, most of the older leaders of Kosei-kai have experienced both sides of her personality: compassion and severity.

Never very strong physically, having received what she considered an extension of her life after an early illness, she splendidly carried out her mission in this world and died at the age of only sixty-eight. Since she left us so early, it is my great regret that I did not stay by her side from an earlier date and profit from the guidance she could have given me.

As many people have pointed out, in religious guidance, Myoko Sensei and father were an excellent combination. Father has described the two of them as the wheels at the ends of the same wagon axle. They supported, encouraged, and instructed each other as they stimulated the development of Kosei-kai and guided many people to salvation. The secret of their success was the complementary nature of their individual roles and the way each was indispensable to the whole of their teaching and guidance. Father taught practical religious action from the standpoint of doctrine. Myoko Sensei taught the same thing but from an emotional standpoint. For this reason, the combined teaching of the Two Sensei, as they were called, was so alive and vital that people said, if cut, it would bleed. The Two Sensei embodied a guidance principle of simultaneous severity and love.

All the leaders, including father and Myoko Sensei, worked day and night to enable Rissho Kosei-kai to grow from an initial group of only thirty members in March 1938, to a membership of over three hundred thousand households on the eve of Myoko Sensei's death. I have heard father often recount how he would pedal his bicycle, Myoko Sensei seated on the rear luggage carrier, on guidance missions that sometimes took them to ten or twenty houses a day. They were both essential to the work. Without their joint efforts, Kosei-kai might never have come into being and certainly would never have become what it is today.

Their combination makes me reflect with amazement on the workings of cause-and-effect relations. From father's standpoint, she was a truly irreplaceable companion in the Law. Hand in hand, encouraging and correcting each other, they were staunch comrades, true to their vow to walk the way of spiritual progress in spite of all interference from without.

LEARNING BY OBSERVING

Though my father and my teacher are one person, as what I have written to this point indicates, I have actually rarely been taught by him in the ordinary educational sense of the word. The lessons I have had and continue to have from him are derived from observing and copying what he does in everyday life. Everything he does, from morning and evening devotional services to such ordinary acts as writing in his diary, is done smoothly and in an apparently spontaneous fashion. When he has an opportunity to do something—for example, study calligraphy or painting—he takes the chance and acts with complete naturalness and with no trace of deliberate effort.

Because of his naturalness, he is always the same, whether at home or in some other place. For instance, he does a great deal of work traveling in connection with a peace movement. When at home, he brings that same talk of peace and its importance to the dinner table, where we all—including both the family members and our domestic help—eat together. His way of understanding and interpreting the Buddha's Law too is natural and in conformity with human life and the flow of time. Since he is not a scholar, he does not insist on adhering to one interpretation but is content with any view, as long as it helps save people.

For example, some time ago there was much lively discussion of the importance of consolidation in our organization and of uniform principles on which to base our thought and action. My younger brother Kinjiro said to father at about that time, "Rissho Kosei-kai enjoys the blessings of the gods, and we ought to have some unified principles that permeate the entire organization." Father said in reply, "In everything I have studied so far, no philosophical principle has appeared to be as outstanding as Buddhism. But, should a finer principle—one that can be put into effective actual practice—come along, I shall be happy to see Kosei-kai embrace it at any time. As president, I myself shall be among the first to adopt it. Matters like uniform principles and consolidated organizations are unimportant. But at present, in terms of teaching and practice, Buddhism is best. And that is why we continue adhering to it.''

The difficulty of meeting and talking with people in foreign lands has led me to develop what might be called an overseas manner, which in turn results in a certain exterior awkwardness in expression and attitude. It is often said that such awkwardness is the product of Japan's long history as an isolated island nation. Father has nothing of this clumsiness at all. He is completely at ease with people anywhere he goes. Unconstrained and relaxed, he preserves his normal mental attitudes under all conditions. And I consider this extraordinary. Often called upon to take part in discussions with learned men for publication in magazines and journals, though modest, he is never cowed by them and preserves balanced composure always. Talking with such people just as he would ordinary guests, he enters into their ways of thinking and absorbs much of great value from the experience.

DEPTH AND BREADTH

Father's faith in the Lotus Sutra was born of the profound emotional impact made on him by lectures he heard from Sukenobu Arai. Profound emotional impact is an important thing, for it is from such feeling that faith germinates. In his case, the teachings of the Lotus Sutra were firmly ingrained in mind and body. During the ten years of his separation from wife and children, he frequently leaped from bed at night to peruse a passage from the sutra or read something in the writings of Nichiren.

I have a book that I keep by my side all the time and read from regularly. It is called *Kiki-seiwa* (Quiet Tales for Times of Crisis), by Masahiro Yasuoka. In it occurs the following passage, which I quote as pertinent to this discussion:

"People today, especially intellectuals, are often said to lack persevering power, the ability to stick to things, drive, and spirit. I think that an enormous cause of this lack is the mistaken belief that textbooks, newspapers, and magazines are omnipotent and infallible. For some time now we Japanese have thought that education is something to be had at school. Conclusion of schooling brings a sense of relief, a gradual lessening in all efforts at learning, and finally limitation of reading to newspapers and magazines. Though we continue to learn our work on the job, bit by bit, we stop learning how to be better human beings. I think the custom in America and other Western countries of calling the termination of university education, not a conclusion, but a commencement—that is, a starting—more accurately indicates what the state of affairs at that stage in human growth ought to be.

"Japanese schooling concentrates solely on textbooks, which are little more than barren compilations of facts. How much of the spirit of a language —one's native tongue or a foreign tongue—can be learned by covering a given number of pages, a certain vocabulary, and a smattering of grammar in a semester? Textbooks on morals, history, ethics, literature, physics, chemistry, and so on deal with their material in the same cold, dry way.

"Books of this kind cannot provide the basic understanding people require. In their place, we should carefully read authoritative works and should constantly read over and over such books as the great Chinese history *Records of the Grand Historian* or the famous Japanese sagas like *Gempei Seisui-ki* [The Rise and Fall of the Minamoto and Taira Clans] and the *Taihei-ki* [Record of the Great Peace]. Unless a person develops the habit of reading them time and time again, the spirits of such works will not transfer themselves to him, and he will not acquire the strength of character he needs. No detailed scholarly interpretations are needed. Even addiction to novel reading is all right, because novels too help us understand what human beings were like in the past and what they are like now. They clarify the principles by which nations are ruled in peace or suffer the disturbances of war; they tell how peoples flourish and how they fall. In short, they reveal how the solemn rules of the human heart and mind come into being. And this is knowledge that we all must have."

Father has read the Lotus Sutra hundreds, even thousands of times. And for this reason, its spirit has transferred itself to him. The sutra has become a matter of living faith, not of mere intellectual understanding for him. This explains why he is never willing to neglect devotional services, even while traveling. Those of us who think we have come to master the sutra because we understand it with our minds realize that missing devotionals a time or two will not detract from our intellectual understanding and therefore easily become lax. Father cannot do this, probably because he has an unconscious, built-in mental warning signal telling him that one day's negligence to religious duties is one day drawn away from faith.

During the construction of the Great Sacred Hall, father spent more than six months copying the Lotus Sutra for inclusion within the statue of Shakyamuni that is enshrined there. He considers this too a highly beneficial undertaking, since it ingrained in his mind not only the meaning but also the very characters of the text. These now rise into his mental eye and serve as a criterion against which to measure all his words and actions.

Some time ago, when Kinjiro complained to father that in spite of three years' effort he was still unable to manifest any mystical powers, father said to him, "First and last, we are all human beings and ought to rely on our own intelligence. People who have mystical powers tend to rely on them too easily.

You have no need of them now. When you have put your own powers of thought to fullest use and still think mystical powers are necessary, then it will be all right to concentrate on attaining them. But if you judge all your actions on the basis of the teachings of the Lotus Sutra, you cannot go wrong."

Having imbued his whole being with what might be called the Lotus Sutra view of the world, father sometimes surprises us. It is customary for a small group of the innermost leaders of our organization to meet in the autumn to discuss policies for the coming year. At one of these gatherings, father said, "Don't devote all our attention to next year's policies for Rissho Kosei-kai alone. Give some thought to the development of other organizations." Kinjiro tells of an occasion when father remarked to the leader of another religious organization that their doctrines were so splendid that they ought to try to win followers all over the island of Kyushu, where Rissho Kosei-kai already has nineteen branches.

Both these instances indicate father's firm belief in the importance of religious cooperation among all groups. Kosei-kai's participation in the Brighter Society Movement and the World Conference on Religion and Peace are still further illustrations of this same belief. Not all Kosei-kai leaders see eye to eye with father on this point. Some have been known to object to these undertakings on the grounds that they disperse our organization's energies, cost money, and offer no immediate positive benefits. But father is unperturbed by what these people say. And, as a true practitioner of the teachings of the Lotus Sutra, he demonstrates the sincerity of a servant of the Buddha as he travels to other religious organizations, to various temples, and even to the Vatican.

TURN TOWARD
THE BUDDHA

I believe that father is always turned toward the Buddha and can always hear the Buddha's voice. Once when he traveled to Europe on the work of the World Conference on Religion and Peace, he was asked by a certain important German religious leader what his qualifications for this work were. Father said, "I have come here on orders from the Buddha. You are a Christian and therefore must hear God's cry for the creation of peace on earth. I have come because I have heard a similar cry from the Buddha." The German religious leader understood at once and immediately agreed to take part in the conference.

Because he is turned always to the gods and the Buddha, father is always sincerely, precisely what he appears to be. His intense honesty sometimes works to his disadvantage. But he does not mind. While those of us around him fret impatiently over it, he laughs, and the disadvantage disappears.

By saying that father is turned toward the gods

and the Buddha, I do not imply that he is in any way what people would call divinely possessed. He has a dislike of anything smacking of blind devotion to the so-called unknown. I recall that at some time during the 1960s a prediction held that a certain miracle would take place on a certain day. We all waited eagerly to see what would happen. Nothing did, even though we clung to the possibility that the miracle might occur before midnight. When the fuss was all over, father cautioned us: "There's no sense in making a lot of careless prophecies. Human beings should exert maximum effort and leave the rest up to the will of heaven. It is insolent to try to foresee what the will of heaven may be. Furthermore, it is all the more wrong, because it can lead people astray."

PERSEVERING IN EVERYTHING

One of the things I am most eager to learn from father is his regularity and methodicalness. He always abides by the rules he ought to keep and does the things he ought to do.

Religious devotionals are the thing he is most regular about. Like other men, father must sometimes be out late at night. He travels and must often leave home very early in the morning. But his schedule is always arranged to give first precedence to his devotionals. This means that if he must leave home at four in the morning he is up in time to perform devotionals and make all other preparations beforehand. He has been doing this for as long as I can recall. Indeed, he has been doing it for longer than I can remember—even when in pain, as he has sometimes been from suspected stomach ulcers—ever since the foundation of Rissho Kosei-kai.

In everything, father sees what he starts through to a satisfactory (to him) end, no matter whether it is regular religious devotionals, calligraphy, or painting. It is not unusual for a person to carry out projects to their terminations. The unusual aspect of father's personality is that he demonstrates this kind of perseverance in absolutely everything.

CARING

Open and optimistic, father is very considerate of others as well. He never forgets kindnesses, even those that go far back in time, and always remembers people at the Bon festival in summer and at New Year, the two most important holidays in the Japanese calendar. Though he wakes early each morning, he suppresses his own desire to rise and lies quietly listening to the radio (a favorite program called "Human Reader") for a while, because if he, the head of the house, got up, the maid, who probably wants a little more sleep, would have to get up too. (Mother is a very early riser. Extremely fond of reading the Lotus Sutra, she usually slips quietly out of bed at four and reads or, if she has time, copies the sutra.)

It seems that father is very considerate of his children too. It may sound odd for me to use the word *seems,* but, as I have said, the special relationship between us deprived me of a chance to experience his parental love directly. In this respect, Kinjiro is more blessed than I am. Kinjiro himself relates the following incident.

"I ate too much good food after the installation ceremony for the focus of devotion in the Great Sacred Hall and that night had a stomachache that kept me awake. Hearing about it, father came and stroked my stomach until, much relieved, I fell asleep. Twenty-five at the time, I was a little shy but very grateful to father for having done what he did to comfort me. The following morning, he told me about sitting by me until I fell asleep before he retired himself and asked how I felt.

"I took the occasion to explain the interpretation I had worked out of father's compassion. I said I realized he wanted us to find true happiness by understanding the Law, abiding by it, and living as it teaches. I added that I thought this was why he lived according to the Law in the family and showed us how to put the Law into practice. To this he replied, 'That's a fine interpretation of a parent's compassion, and I hate to sound like a spoilsport. But the truth is that your education is not on my mind at all when

I try to live according to the Law. I have lived and continue to live this way out of gratitude for the way the Lotus Sutra explains that a given action produces such and such an effect. Once I found out the truth of this relation, I could not live any other way.'

"To tell the truth, I was shocked. I had thought for the first time I truly understood father's compassion and expected him to put his arm around my shoulder and compliment me on having seen the truth at last, after twenty-five years. Suddenly, to my amazement I realized how far off track I was.

"But, on reflection, I saw that father's kind of compassion is stern and unsentimental, as this incident proved."

After a meeting of the Japanese Committee of the World Conference on Religion and Peace, held on Mount Hiei, not far from Kyoto, back at the hotel in the city, father announced his desire to arrange a dinner party for the reporters, cameramen, and secretaries covering the conference. It was suggested that everyone go out to a restaurant, but once again father demonstrated his concern and caring for others by insisting that the party be held in the hotel. His reason was that if they went out the chauffeur, who always worked hard, would have to refrain from drinking and having as good a time as he might have. Father often helps photographers and secretaries with their baggage when they accompany him on his trips abroad. If a group of men is standing in line waiting for an elevator and a woman comes up, father will tap them on the shoulder and ask them to step aside and let her board ahead of them: ladies first.

Customarily, we enjoy some sakè with our evening meal, but father calls a halt at the right time because he does not want to keep the people in the kitchen waiting to clean up.

IMPARTIALITY

Those of us who are with him a great deal know that father is not the kind of person who lets his position as the leader of a large organization go to his head. There are people who allow their personal authority to influence not only their attitudes but also their very manner of speaking with others. Father speaks to everyone on the same level. He says what must be said without abbreviation and without pulling punches. He shares the things he finds unusual and interesting and the things that make him happy with all members of the household. When he comes home from international travels, he always has plenty to tell. And we find his stories so interesting that on his homecoming nights the whole family, including Kinjiro and Hiroshi and their wives and children, assembles with us for dinner. Meals at such times are noisy and fun, since there are always cousins at the house to fill out the table.

Everyone is dear to father, and he is impartial to all, not only to his own children and grandchildren but to Kosei-kai leaders and members too. I am confident that I can be as free and equal with others as father, though I have a long way to go before I can truly reach the level of impartiality that he commands.

ABILITY, PERSEVERANCE, AND EFFORT

Once, as father watched from the veranda of our house, Kinjiro and I tried to roll an unwieldy, oddly shaped stone that refused to go where we wanted it to go. "Wait, let me show you how," father called. Taking a pole, he used it as a lever to maneuver the stone where we wanted it. He must have learned how to do this while working as a gardener's apprentice when a young man. He learned many other things too in his youth and long years of varied experience. For instance, though today he himself goes to *shiatsu* massage specialists for therapy, I remember when he used to massage mother and me and bring great relief to our weary or aching bodies. This knowledge he acquired from his father. His home village was without a doctor of any kind in the past, and the Niwano family—especially my great-grandfather and grandfather—were local healers. Father learned from them. He seems to know how to do anything, and I marvel at all he has absorbed as a result of years of experience, especially since I am exactly the opposite.

My experience of the world cannot compare with his for richness and variety. He was a member of a fire-fighting squad. In wintertime in the country he learned how to spin flaxen thread for a famous local cloth. In the summer he worked as a laborer on a dam project not far from home. At the age of seventeen, he traveled to Tokyo, where he worked for a rice merchant, a landscape gardener, a charcoal dealer, and a pickle dealer. Later he ran a milk store and served in the navy. In religious matters too he has an extensive background. He was a member of the Organization of National Faith and Virtue, studied the eclectic Buddhist Shugen-do system of asceticism in an organization called Tengu-fudo, learned name interpretation under Seiko Kobayashi, and studied the Lotus Sutra in the Reiyu-kai association. Thereafter he went on to found Rissho Kosei-kai. Though I was sent to school for twenty-four years in comparison to his six, in no realm is my experience comparable with his. Aside from helping in the fields during the years we spent in Suganuma, I never worked and never earned any money on my own.

Since he has grown older he customarily takes a nap in the afternoon unless duties prevent. He says it is good for his health and considers it rude to look sleepy in front of other people. But I have never seen him merely lounge about casually. For his naps, he has the Japanese bedding spread in the proper manner. "Sleeping too is a kind of discipline," he insists. A part of that discipline is making certain that one gets the required amount of sound sleep. He says that the night before explains why people sometimes find it difficult to get up on time in the morning. No matter how tempting the television may be—and father has things he likes to watch, too, especially contact sports like sumo wrestling, boxing, kickboxing, and Western-style wrestling, which he finds a totally engrossing change of pace and relaxation from his heavy daily schedule of meetings—when a person has to rise early, he must go to bed early enough to enable him to get up when he must.

Sleep is good for the health, and so is exercise. For the sake of improving his physical condition, at the age of fifty-eight, father started playing golf. If I may be permitted to boast about him, he got to the point that he has a twelve handicap. Lately, however, his heavy schedule has kept him from playing much.

The mention of golf calls to mind an instance in which father scolded me and Kinjiro for not knowing when enough is enough. One year, at New Year vacation time, Kinjiro, Hiroshi, and I went out for a game of golf and, when it was over, decided to go to Kinjiro's to play mahjong. I was to go home first to get the mahjong set and then go on to Kinjiro's. But when I got home and told father of our plans, he scolded me by saying, "You boys never get enough. Playing is all right, but limit yourselves to one kind of amusement a day. You want to go on and on without stop. You don't know how to call it quits." After this, I found it hard to go to my brother's, and, worried that I was so late, he called home only to receive the same admonition from father that I had gotten.

Though he cautions in this way, father never tells me or any other member of the family what we must or must not do. I suppose this is because he thinks people will not persevere in anything they do not willingly undertake on their own.

When I observe father, who had no more formal education than is available in a country school, reading difficult books, writing with the skill of a calligrapher, and painting pictures, I realize that though he certainly must have ability to do these things he also has the will to persevere and to make the effort necessary to master a subject or skill.

Though he turned seventy-five last fall, father is still hale and hearty. One day during the New Year holidays two years ago he played golf on one course, while Kinjiro and Hiroshi were playing on another. When they later compared scores, it turned out that father was tops. And he did not hesitate to let them know about it. I should say at this point that golf is the only thing that ever keeps father from work. He is extraordinarily industrious and goes to his office at Kosei-kai headquarters even on days following his return from overseas.

BIGNESS

Father's nature is so big that he sometimes looks gullible. As I have said, he deals with everyone on the same level and never doubts anyone. (This occasionally causes anxiety for the rest of us.) Completely lacking vanity, self-importance, and timidity he frankly announces to all that he is the son of a poor farmer with little formal education. Always smiling and open and never position-proud, he immediately attracts and wins over everyone who talks with him, even those people who entertain doubts about him before their first encounter. The scale of his personality is illustrated by the success with which he teaches. The rest of us can explain the Lotus Sutra assiduously and still fail to enable our audiences to understand. Father says a few words, and his listeners grasp the meaning immediately. Another element that enables father to display great convincing powers is the profound faith he has in what he is doing. This saw him through the difficult decade of separation from wife and children and through the hardships and trials that have befallen Rissho Kosei-kai since its founding. At that time, father and the other leaders of the organization vowed never to give up their faith in the Lotus Sutra. Mother made the same vow, and it provided her and father with sustaining strength during the years they were apart. We other members of the family now have this kind of faith but arrived at it and at an understanding of father and of Kosei-kai only after we had methodically studied the Lotus Sutra. Our apparently circuitous route must have been the result of karma or predestination.

Father never deliberately instructs us or tries to influence our decisions. I have never had any advice from him on how to lead people and have been instructed by him directly only on those occasions when I asked him what to say and how to act on trips to Kosei-kai chapters in outlying districts.

The ten years of separation, the years of living like strangers though under the same roof, and then the decision that I must inherit his position in the organization still exert an influence on relations between father and me. I have never entrusted my whole naked self to him, and he has always maintained reserve in connection with me. Even when we are watching the same television program, he looks at a set in one room and I at a set in another. Mother and my wife ask why we do not use the same television; but I object, and father never suggests that we watch together. He believes in letting things take their natural course and never imposes his own will. I too believe in letting things go their natural ways. But whereas he is positive in his approach, I am negative.

Nonetheless, where I am concerned, father takes a negative stance. For instance, some time ago, I fell while ice-skating at Komagatake, in Hakone, and injured my left wrist. In the lodge dining hall father looked at my bandaged arm and asked what the matter was. I merely said I had hurt myself. Later, he found out the details from my wife. Indeed, since we maintain mutual distance from each other, we often communicate through my wife. When I have something I want to find out from father, I ask her to ask him and then get his answer from her. He often makes comments about our actions and words through her. My wife is interested in name interpretation and fortune interpretation on the basis of directions and frequently consults with father on these matters. Because I do not wish my mind to develop fixed ideas about these or other interpretations of fate, I prefer to remain aloof from them. And this puts still more distance between father and me. To an outsider, we must seem a very strange father-son pair. But, actually, he has an eye on me all the time, and I am constantly observing him.

TRIAL AND RESPONSE

All the members of our organization are accustomed to seeing father smiling and beamingly talking with complete composure no matter how tired he is. At home, too, he never shouts or scowls, and his face wrinkles with delight when he is called granddaddy by my four daughters. But he has undergone trials and hardships too. And I should like to give my impressions of what probably took place in his mind as he underwent them.

His first serious trial in connection with Rissho Kosei-kai took place in 1943, five years after the organization's founding. In those days a notorious piece of legislation called the Peace Preservation Law allowed the government to imprison people for reasons that today seem absurd. On March 13 of that year, a policeman appeared at Kosei-kai headquarters and ordered father to accompany him to police headquarters. Father was charged with corrupting people's minds through religious teaching and was put in jail, where he remained for two weeks. During this time many leading officers left the organization. Though father has never been one to chase after people who have decided to go and though he claims to have been totally cool and collected in jail, there can be no doubt that he suffered when he thought of the futures of the roughly one thousand households whose religious lives depended on him at that time. The outcome of this misfortune was happy, however, since it resulted in a stable organizational arrangement with father as president and Myoko Naganuma as vice-president.

Pilgrimages to a holy mountain called Shichimen and to Mount Minobu, where the great thirteenth-century Buddhist leader Nichiren lived part of his life and the location of the head temple of one of the largest branches of the sect that bears his name, were begun two years after the inception of Kosei-kai and remained a tradition for fifteen years. Then trips to Mount Minobu were halted. Rissho Kosei-kai reveres the Lotus Sutra and chants what is called the *Daimoku* (the invocation "Hail to the Sutra of the Lotus Flower of the Wonderful Law"), as do adherents of the Nichiren sect. In 1952, father proposed to the head Nichiren temple on Mount Minobu that all people, lay and clerical alike, who put their trust in the Lotus Sutra and chant the *Daimoku* should band together in one vast movement. The policies that he advanced were unity of doctrines, unity of focus of devotion, and unity of dissemination methods. But, perhaps because Kosei-kai membership numbered only thirty-two thousand households at the time, Mount Minobu not only rejected the idea but also barred the entire Kosei-kai from the Nichiren sect. Our organization became in the spiritual and physical senses totally independent.

After this great trial, father had nothing to rely on but the true Law itself. But the very act of requesting unification with the Nichiren sect demonstrates the size and resilience of father's mind. It is rare for the head of a religious sect to make such a request. Father was able to do this because he has never felt that Kosei-kai alone is right or that it is the only organization promising salvation. Other religious doctrines too include the truth. They manifest themselves in different organizations and forms because of the different karmas of their members. The only thing that is important is earnestness and sincerity. Forced, while desiring unification, to undergo debarment, father must have despaired. But today, our organization holds no animosity against Mount Minobu.

In 1956, the *Yomiuri Shimbun,* one of the largest and most influential newspapers in Japan, started a violent campaign against Kosei-kai that lasted two months, beginning on January 25, and that occupied a great deal of column space daily. The scandal caused consternation among the membership. Since some people still harbored strong prejudices against new religious organizations in those days, the paper was able to print accusations that Kosei-kai was a wicked sect, and, believing what they read, new members or people of less than staunch faith became so upset that they left the group. In fact, during the year of the *Yomiuri* campaign, about seventy thousand households did drop out of Rissho Kosei-kai. Leaders of our organization suggested suing the paper, since its accusations were totally groundless. But father said a religious group must not engage in battles. Instead, he called on members to think of the *Yomiuri Shimbun* as a bodhisattva mercifully providing all of them with an excellent chance to reflect on their own failings. The whole incident had a stimulating effect on the growth and solidarity of young members.

At the time, father had three heavy loads of suffering to bear. First, of course, was the campaign by the *Yomiuri Shimbun,* second were our own domestic problems, and third—and this is the one father himself calls most grievous—was a campaign of petitions against him circulated within Kosei-kai. For over twenty years, the very mention of these petitions was taboo. I came to know of them fully when I read father's complete autobiography, published in Japanese in 1976. Since only a very limited number of leaders had known about them, the revelation shocked many members. Though all of the Kosei-kai leaders compiled these petitions and forced them on him, father considered them a discipline granted him by the Buddha to enable him to rid himself of laziness and pride. To this day, he holds no grudge about the matter.

The petitions started in about 1954 and continued until 1957. Mother and the rest of us returned from Suganuma in 1954 and for the next three years, while the petitions were being circulated, lived with father as strangers under one roof. Every day at headquarters father was treated coldly by the leaders. If he went to Myoko Sensei's house, he would find the front door locked. He was told that, since some of the membership was losing confidence in him, mother would not be permitted to join Kosei-kai.

This critical attitude toward him had been in the air from the year before our return to Tokyo. Every day at headquarters must have been like walking on pins and needles for father. This may explain why he could not enjoy family life and why he could not join us around one table at mealtimes but, upon coming home and paying his respects before the family altar, went immediately upstairs and did not come down again. I suspect that he suffered and punished himself alone every day in the determined effort to attain enlightenment. By censuring himself he sublimated his resentments and dislikes.

And, if my guess about what he endured at the time is correct, I was guilty of terrible lack of consideration in willfully inflicting further punishment on him. Whatever the facts in this connection, however, sufferings made father bigger, and I was raised by this still bigger man. Today, my wife and children and I live in the room where he underwent and responded to all those trials in the past.

OPENING OTHERS' MINDS

Though I took part as an observer in the first World Conference on Religion and Peace, in Kyoto, and in the second, held in Louvain, Belgium, I was first an actual representative at the conference when it was held at Princeton Theological Seminary, in the United States, in August and September 1979. As inexperienced as I am, I was hesitant to shoulder this great burden. But father is prevented from representing Rissho Kosei-kai in the Japanese committee, since he is president of the committee, and I agreed. There had been a request from the Japanese committee too for me to accept this responsibility. My wife accompanied me. In addition to the conference, we attended celebrations of the twentieth anniversary of the Los Angeles Kosei-kai branch, congratulatory ceremonies and rites for the installation of a focus of devotion at the San Francisco branch, and twentieth-anniversary ceremonies at the Hawaii branch.

While attending the conference at Princeton, I became convinced that father is right when he tells our members that Japan and the Japanese must serve as models for the whole world today. After opening prayers at Saint Patrick's Cathedral, we three hundred and fifty conferees visited the United Nations, where I was greatly impressed by the hopes this organization of a hundred and fifty-seven nations puts in our private group and the contributions it can make to true peace. In other words, national governments are beginning to put their trust in a private group of lay people. Awareness of this brought powerfully back some other words father has taught me: "The discipline and training of the lay believer represent the way Buddhists ought to work for true peace. Discipline and training consist in saving other people who live and suffer in the grime of the same world we all inhabit. This is the meaning of real salvation."

Only a little over a year earlier, in June 1978, father had made a speech in the name of peace at the United Nations. (To my immense joy, he was the first representative of a religious body like the World

Conference on Religion and Peace ever to do so.) On the hot August day of our visit, the room in which our meeting was held was insufficiently air-conditioned, and I recall how refreshing my glass of ice water was. I was disturbed, however, to see that not everyone in the room received ice water.

At Princeton, meetings lasted from seven in the morning till eleven at night, when special committee gatherings concluded their day's work. Many of the nearly four hundred conferees from over thirty nations were of advanced ages, but, enjoying the presence of their God or Buddha, they were all cheerful and energetic and ate with appetites that surprised us younger people.

Father too was always smiling, especially when he met friends from former conferences. Though they spoke in languages father does not understand, even if no interpreter was on hand, all the people he talked to spoke warmly and affectionately, often holding his hand as they engaged in a kind of communion of the mind that transcends words. Father has a wonderful and totally natural ability to lead people out in this way, to open their minds to a wider, deeper communication.

In some opinions the highlight and one of the greatest achievements of the conference was an invitation to meet President and Mrs. Carter at the White House. To my way of thinking, however, even in America, which is supposed to be a land of freedom and equality, the White House represents a citadel of authority. Furthermore, I was not especially thrilled at the meeting because I think we have our work to do as people of religion and that Mr. Carter had his as president. Still, both the president and first lady were especially hospitable to my wife, shook her hand several times, and had a photograph taken with her.

On our way home, we stopped at the Grand Canyon and visited Salt Lake City. All of this was valuable experience for me. Still, particularly because of my lack of ease with foreign languages (my wife, who speaks some English, got along better in this connection than I did and had a better time as a result), I was happy to be back in Japan among a people that, I am certain, has an important role to play in contributing to peace for the whole world.

As I draw to the end of this book, I should like to take note of a few things that serve as guidelines in certain aspects of daily living and that symbolize my aspirations. The first is a set of maxims by the philosopher and healer Haruchika Noguchi that I once read at a meeting of Kosei-kai leaders. Some of his wise words are very pertinent to me, especially when they warn against over-cautiousness (I have already said that I am the kind who taps on a stone bridge before stepping on it to make sure it is sound).

"The person who thinks, 'This piece of work will wear me out,' gets tired.

"The person who thinks, 'This is too much for me,' can never accomplish the task.

"The person who thinks, 'This will be hard to do unless I really put my shoulder to it,' will find the job hard to do.

"But the person who goes ahead and does it wholeheartedly gets the work done with ease.

"The person who believes he can do it will be perplexed.

"The person who thinks, 'I'll do this as soon as I have the strength,' will never do it.

"The person who is confident he can do it all alone will fail.

"The person who desperately feels compelled to undertake the task will rush and be frustrated.

"But the person who wholeheartedly goes ahead, telling himself all the while that this is the way to do it, will gain strength.

"That is how life is. That is how human nature is. The person who wants to do something cannot. The person who believes he can do something fails. But the person who goes ahead and does it grows stronger and accomplishes what he sets out do to.

"The person who is frank about his inner needs never wearies. His strength is within. The more he uses it, the more it grows, and the stronger he becomes. Unused, strength rusts and fades away.

"We must all make bold, full use of the powers we have. . . ."

"The person who says, 'I will do thus and so when I have recovered from this illness,' will do nothing even after recovery. The person, who, though ill, rises and acts recovers good health. . . ."

"The ever-cautious person will sooner or later suffer for his caution. He will cause his own powers to shrivel. . . ."

"Constant use of inner power to best advantage keeps human beings healthy and amplifies their strength. . . ."

"Human beings' inner power is connected with infinity, using it cannot diminish it. . . ."

Second, I should like to develop as quickly as possible the mental fluidity and flexibility illustrated by the metaphor of water in the following two Sung-dynasty Chinese poems.

> The stream is abandoned to its flow
> Though all around stays still.
> Flowers fall in profusion
> Though all the mood is calm.
> —Shao K'ang-chieh

> The stream bounds from canyon walls
> Wishing to vie with none.
> The moon sheds light on a thousand hills
> Itself remaining alone.
> —Lin Chu-hsien

As these poems suggest, no matter how turbulent and tumultuous life is, the human mind must remain calm. Life is hard, and one's true self must be something shining above mundane affairs. Without struggle and without being overwhelmed by the things of the world, one must remain always calm. This is the mute message of these poems and the state I hope to attain.

POSTSCRIPT

Some time ago, worried about our inability to approach believers with the same assurance he has, Kinjiro and I asked father if we ought to try to undergo the same kind of severe discipline and training he and other founding members of Rissho Kosei-kai underwent. His reply is important and pregnant with suggestions not only for me and my brother but for all members of our organization as well:

"Myoko Sensei and I and the others who worked to get Kosei-kai started had our own experiences, but nothing says you must undergo the same kind of discipline we knew. If you did, you would be able to save only people of our generations who would share the views such discipline presupposes.

"Times change. Life styles change. Value criteria alter and diversify. People in positions of leadership must keep up with all these changes. Of course, the essentials of Buddhism are eternal and immutable, but the ways they are put to use and applied must suit the needs of the times and the audience. This is what we mean by limitless experience.

"We older members are the roots of Kosei-kai. The trunk is now standing, and you younger people must become the branches, leaves, flowers, and fruit. You don't have to train yourselves to be roots and trunks. These parts of the tree are already there, and all you have to do is accept them and go on with your own jobs. You will have to suffer too. But your kind of suffering will differ from ours. You will have to face new, complicated problems and will have to put your lives on the line in solving them.

"Basically, the issues will be similar, but the problems will manifest themselves in new ways. This means that though, fundamentally it will be the same, your discipline will have novel nuances. Don't be foolish enough to lack confidence because you have not trained yourselves as we trained ourselves. As I have said, the roots and trunk are ready. You have the duties of putting forth branches that culminate in fruit. Have the confidence required for your task and train yourselves to be able to fulfill it."

Father's message for all of us is this. We of the younger generations must approach our work from a different angle. He, Myoko Sensei, and the other senior leaders of our organization believed in serving others for the sake of their own salvation. Now, at a time when they have already laid the foundations for us, we must come to realize that our faith exists for the sake of bringing happiness to as many other people as possible.

BQ 8389 .N547 A3713 1982

Niwano, Nichik⁻o, 1938-

My father, my teacher

ISSUED TO

BQ 8389 .N547 A3713 1982

Niwano, Nichik⁻o, 1938-

My father, my teacher

DEMCO